TASTE & SEE

Awakening Our Spiritual Senses

TIM DEARBORN

InterVarsity Press
Downers Grove, Illinois

InterVarsity Press® is the book-publishing division of InterVarsity Christian Fellowship®, a student movement active on campus at hundreds of universities, colleges and schools of nursing in the United States of America, and a member movement of the International Fellowship of Evangelical Students. For information about local and regional activities, write Public Relations Dept., InterVarsity Christian Fellowship, 6400 Schroeder Rd., P.O. Box 7895, Madison, WI 53707-7895.

All Scripture quotations, unless otherwise indicated, are taken from the HOLY BIBLE, NEW INTERNATIONAL VERSION®. NIV®. Copyright © 1973, 1978, 1984 by International Bible Society. Used by permission of Zondervan Publishing House. All rights reserved.

Cover photograph: Charlie Waite
ISBN 0-8308-1985-1

Printed in the United States of America ∞

Library of Congress Cataloging-in-Publication Data

Dearborn, Tim.
    Taste and see: awakening our spiritual senses/Tim Dearborn.
        p.   cm.
    Includes bibliographical references (p.).
    ISBN 0-8308-1985-1 (pbk.: alk. paper)
        1. Spiritual life—Christianity. 2. Dearborn, Tim. 3. Christian
    life—Presbyterian authors. I. Title.
    BV4501.2.D412   1996
    230—dc20   96-16318
                                                              CIP

17   16   15   14   13   12   11   10   9   8   7   6   5   4   3   2   1
10   09   08   07   06   05   04   03   02   01   00   99   98   97   96

To Kerry, Alison, Andrea and Bethany,
my soulmate, family, allies and companions
in the Pilgrimage;
to Bruce and Hazel Larson,
who have been my mentors and advocates;
and to our friends in Banchory, Scotland,
who have shown us the power of Christian community
as deliciously appetizing, tangible truth.

1
The Pursuit of Truth We Can Touch

WE LIVE IN A SENSORY-ORIENTED, SPIRITUALLY STARVING WORLD. FOR TWO CEN-ries the Western world tried to convince itself that it could survive and indeed thrive as a "secular society." We now know that we can't! The power of the myth of secularism is broken. Yet the ravages of secularism have left us, its victims, with evacuated souls and hungry hearts. We know that we're not alone, and that there's a spiritual dimension to life. We long to encounter spiritual, eternal reality in the midst of our material, time-bound world.

In response to the resurgent "market" for religion, the religious marketplace has become saturated with fiercely competitive marketers of "spiritual" truths. Paralleling the competitive marketing of fast-food restaurants, whose neon signs dominate the decor on our urban avenues, spiritual self-help systems, soothsayers, diviners and gurus peddle their wares throughout our cities.

To make matters more complicated, we're not sure how to evaluate all the advertisements for various "spiritual products" which we receive. We have grown so accustomed to regarding religion as the domain of personal opinion that we've lost any corporate and rational criteria for recognizing eternal truth. We've come to believe that the only valid criteria that can be used to assess the value of religious beliefs are opinions and experiences. So how can we distinguish between junk mail and important personal correspondence? How do we discern between false and true claims? Everyone's experience seems equally valid.

Like spiritual sleepwalkers emerging from a tormented slumber, we've lost our bearings and are finding it hard to distinguish reality from fantasy amid the many voices clamoring for our attention.

Nothing is more urgently needed than *visible theology*—the knowledge of God made evident to our eyes and ears, hands and hearts. We long for an encounter with the eternal God here on earth, in a way that we can taste and see. In spite of being sated by sensory stimuli, our hunger remains unquenched, and we long for solid spiritual food. Yet the resurgence of religious fundamentalism and violent pretenders for the throne of God on earth terrifies us. If these are eternal truth made visible, eternity looks more like a nightmare than a sweet dream.

This book offers an account of highlights of my route as I've pursued and been pursued by tangible truth. It is more a chart for pilgrims than a treatise for theologians. It's a primer for those who are seeking to sink spiritual roots into graciously nourishing soil. It is not intended as a contribution to the academic debates that are fodder for formally trained theologians. Rather, it is trail food for the hungry pilgrim who is looking for theological nourishment. Nevertheless, it is written without fear of theology. In fact, I believe that pastors and seminary professors have erroneously misjudged laypersons, assuming that the laity are terrified of the "T-word"—theology.

Theology, once lauded as the queen of sciences, has fallen into disrepute and disrepair. It has often been ensnared in the esoteric, in arguments about the construction and deconstruction of words and in overly simplifying systems of logic. Actually, theology is quite simply the study of God. If there is a God, and if this God is both good and true, then there is no topic more worthy of our study. We all hunger for knowledge of God. What a tragedy, then, that in the eyes of many, theology has been disrobed of its life-giving vitality by intellectual strippers. It has been shut out from the warmth of everyday sunlight and been overexposed to the surgical lights of intellectual debates and mind games. I believe that God never intended it to be so.

True Christian theology is alive and life-giving. How can living people relate to the living God through a dead medium? God has intended that our knowledge of him be a living knowledge, involving our whole life. Israel expresses this in its ancient *Shema:* "Hear, O Israel: The LORD our God, the LORD is one. Love the LORD your God with all your heart and with all your soul and with all your strength" (Deut 6:4-5). We know God with our whole lives and selves—not just with our minds. Since we know God as embodied people, our theology can't help but be embodied.

So theology is not about grand abstractions and airy speculations, but about food, drink, friendship and all the other ordinary elements of our everyday lives. Theology, as it turns out, is intensely practical, and all practice has intense theological implications.

Catching Our Attention Through Crises

It would be nice to think that our religious life is guided by keen intellectual insights and provoked by thoughtful passion. But the reality is that the deepening of our pursuit of God is usually propelled by crises.

I was one of those reluctant converts who are dragged kicking and screaming into the kingdom. Because I am a thick-skulled, stubbornly slow learner, God has sometimes had to resort to the dramatic to capture my attention. Out of the many attention-grabbing high points in my spiritual pilgrimage, the following three events illustrate the mercy that comes through crisis, as well as the eternal value of crises as triggers for growth. Crises provoke adrenaline, adrenaline stimulates our senses, and thus crises can be wondrous opportunities for being awakened to the tangibility of truth.

A social crisis. My "religious awakening" was triggered by a social crisis. As a high-school student I was dragged along to a church youth group retreat, motivated as much by interest in the female members of the group as by the allure of the gospel. I was definitely not yet Christian.

To close the retreat, all of us crowded into a small chapel and sat in front of a table dotted with little cups of Welch's grape juice and chopped-up bits of bread. I had been told this was going to be "supper," but it didn't even look to me like very good appetizers. The minister leading the retreat droned on, making a big deal about this "feast"—and in so doing confirming to me what strange eyesight Christians have. He talked about the juice as blood and the bread crumbs as the body of Jesus Christ.

I wasn't even convinced that Christ had ever lived, and now I was supposed to believe chopped-up French bread was his body. Even more, we were supposed to eat his body and drink his blood! I felt like I was being introduced to a cannibalistic ritual of a secret society, and didn't know whether to flee the room or sit still. I looked around at my friends, incredulous that they actually believed this tale.

Before I could decide what to do, the plate of bread crumbs passed before me—and suddenly I sensed there was more to this meal than poorly prepared hors d'oeuvres. Not knowing what was going on, but sensing for the first time in my life a meeting point between my broken humanity and God's healing divinity, I ate and drank.

A little bite of French bread and a few drops of grape juice. Strange vessels for an encounter with the infinite God. Yet I sensed something hidden beneath or within these ordinary foodstuffs. My appetite was whetted. I hungered for more.

A medical crisis. God met me, and continues to meet me, in my hunger. Years after my conversion, in the midst of my first pastoral ministry, I needed another awakening. It's easy for pastors to let their ministry substitute for spirituality. Because all of one's attention is supposedly focused on serving God, it is assumed that one is focusing on God himself. Because all one does is supposedly done in the name of God, one must be doing it for God. Nothing is more misleading than these presumptuous assumptions. God helped me discover my spiritual vacuity in the midst of a boating accident.

It was meant to be a tranquil Sunday-morning tour of the bay in a college boat. I was serving as chaplain at a Presbyterian college in Sitka, Alaska, and had seized the rare opportunity offered by a beautiful sunny day to take my sister-in-law, who was helping us following the birth of our first child, to see our breathtaking scenery.

The eagles soared, and the snow-capped mountains shone. God was indeed showing off his creativity. However, I was too busy pointing out the splendors to notice a small "rogue" wave. Our flat-bowed boat smashed into it. I was knocked into the seat in front of me, which took my breath away more literally than had the vistas.

As I caught my breath and my sister-in-law and I picked ourselves up, she reassured me that she was OK. But I wasn't! I restarted the motor and headed for the dock. By the time I reached shore, all I could do was crawl up the gangway.

An ambulance arrived to take me to the hospital, and fortunately the one surgeon in town wasn't out fishing. By the time he'd operated to remove my ruptured spleen and tape up my broken ribs, I had lost half my blood through internal bleeding. Another few minutes and I would have been dead.

Lacking a blood bank, the hospital put out a call on the local radio station for blood donations. Soon the entire town knew that the chaplain had been playing hooky from church!

That evening when I awoke from surgery, rather than being flooded with gratitude to God for sparing my life, I was actually angry. "God, how could you let me almost die? Our long-awaited first child is only one month old. I'm in the midst of my first pastoral ministry, after years of preparation. You're blessing this campus, and wonderful changes are occurring in the lives of students. I have before me all my hopes and dreams for the future. How could you let this almost happen?"

God's word penetrated my morphine-soaked brain with shattering clarity. "What is this 'almost died' talk? You died nine years ago, when as an eighteen-year-old you gave your life to me!" And then the words of Galatians 2:20 came to mind, and in the almost two decades that have passed since that day, I haven't been able to get away from those words.

If any passage is my life verse, this is it. "I have been crucified with Christ and I no longer live, but Christ lives in me. The life I live in the body, I live by faith in the Son of God, who loved me and gave himself for me."

Every day I touch a six-inch-long "icon" that reminds me of this truth: a scar along my stomach, the remnant of the accident that ruptured my spleen. This for me, is tangible truth.

A vocational crisis. Sadly, even such a dramatically awakened awareness can quickly fade. It took a vocational crisis to recapture my attention and redirect my life.

After several years in Alaska, our three-person family moved to Seattle, where I served as the pastor of missions at University Presbyterian Church. God gave us the opportunity there to learn from his people throughout the world. On one trip to Haiti, I asked a dynamic Haitian pastor my favorite question for non-Western Christians: "What are the qualities of a good missionary?" I'll never forget his reply.

"A good missionary is someone who loves Jesus, and who loves Haitians!" Simple, yet penetrating.

"How many missionaries do you know in Haiti?" I asked.

"About two hundred," he replied.

"How many good ones?"

He reflected for a minute and then said, "About ten."

"Don't get me wrong," he continued. "I'm sure all the rest are trying to love Jesus and are trying to learn how to love us Haitians. But what they really express to us is that they are primarily here to fulfill their own career objectives. They're here to dig wells, plant churches, enable agricultural reform, evangelize, staff orphanages, provide medical care. Those are all great goals. We need all of that, and more! Yet we sense that for them, Jesus and we Haitians are means to the fulfillment of their own ambitions."

All the way home on the plane I reflected on that conversation: "Jesus and we are means to the fulfillment of their own career ambitions!" God used these words to redirect my gaze. I realized that I was not very different from those missionaries. My ambitions may have been noble and maybe even sanctified. But in a very real sense I was using the church where I was a pastor to satisfy my agenda. I wanted to see a church become as committed to God's purposes in the world as it was to God's purposes in its own building. I had prayed and pushed, ministered and manipulated so that my church would be as concerned about providing a building for a church in Kenya as about repairing its own roof. Providing Sunday school for Cambodian children in Seattle should become as passionate a desire as providing for our own children.

God was honoring all these efforts in our church. Through the prayer, witness and involvement of many people, mission was moving from the church's periphery, as the domain of a few eccentrics, to its heart and core, taken up as the passion of the people of God. But at what cost? Though others might not have seen it, I realized that I was becoming like the ravenous wolves of whom Jesus spoke in Matthew 7. I may have looked good on the outside, all dressed up in sheep's clothing. But inside I bordered on devouring people to see my goals met.

One day when I stood before the Lord, would I echo the dialogue Jesus describes at the end of Matthew 7? Would I say, "Lord, Lord, look at all the miracles I performed in your name, look at the sermons I preached and the demons I cast out"?

Would the Lord say, "Depart from me, I don't know who you are"?

For years following that airborne crisis, my wife and I partook weekly of the Lord's Supper together in our home. I realized that if I approach life and ministry spiritually hungry, then I am dangerous. If I serve in order to have my ambitions satisfied, then my service will ultimately be unsatisfactory. I dare not engage in ministry spiritually hungry, lest I devour others to satisfy my unmet needs.

Recently my wife and I happened to encounter a missionary passing through our city on his way back from India. Over ten years earlier he and his wife had stayed in our home and had been present for our weekly Communion. So many years later, he commented that our shared Lord's Supper had made an unforgettable impression on him.

The root issue in spiritual growth isn't discipline and determination but desire and hunger. For whom am I living—for my own fears and hopes or for our Lord? For what am I hungry—for success and affirmation or for our Lord? The only satisfying answer to both questions is the same—the Lord Jesus Christ.

God is at work in every moment of our lives to draw us to our deeper desires, to awaken our most healthy hungers, and through that to lead us to himself, to his tangible truth.

Bringing Truth to Life

At the heart of our hunger for tangible truth is a desire to be touched by love. Most radio stations would go out of business if there weren't songs about love. Greeting-card companies would be bankrupt; floral shops would close; our wedding, funeral and gift-giving industries would wither. With good reason, love is something we sing, write, give and grieve over. The English poet Thomas Traherne may have said it correctly when he wrote, "We are as prone to love as the sun is to shine, it being the most natural and delightful employment of the soul of mankind." Nevertheless, none of us are very good lovers.

The warfare that divides dozens of nations, that makes some of our city streets unsafe for human habitation and that turns many of our own homes into battlefields stands as a glaring indictment of our failure as lovers. Even as Christians, we love to talk, sing and even shout about love, yet we're not experts at living it. Twenty-eight thousand denominations! Several hundred new ones every month! Churches laden by schisms, suspicion and separation by race, class and custom stand as signs over which the world mocks us for our lovelessness. Scripture also holds us in judgment, as we read in 1 John 3:18-19, "Let us not love with words or tongue but with actions and in truth. This then is how we know that we belong to the truth." The assurance of our orthodoxy is found not merely in our doctrines but in our deeds of love!

Yet merely to command us to be more loving is as pointless as to ask people from some of the rival ethnic groups that are embroiled in long-term warfare to stop fighting, or to tell a divorcing couple that it would be nice if they got along. It's not that simple. We're not very good at loving ourselves, let alone others. Our struggle with self-image, self-acceptance and self-worth keeps millions of therapists employed and thousands of recovery groups fully enrolled. We long to put our fractured selves back together and to drown out the accusations that haunt us.

Once again John speaks to us, saying that when we act in love, "we set our hearts at rest in his presence whenever our hearts condemn us. For God is greater than our hearts, and he knows everything" (1 Jn 3:19-20). There's an unquestionable universal longing for hearts that are at rest, for an end to the accusations that haunt us. John indicates that the solution is easy—simply act in love.

But living the solution isn't easy. Deep within us is a resistance to love, because we can't really believe that we (or for that matter, very many other people) are lovable.

Longing for Our Parents' Pleasure

All of us long for our parents' affirmation. We live listening for the words "I'm proud of you." If we've never heard that, and we've not grown beyond pursuit of our parents' pleasure, we're likely to feel relentlessly dissatisfied and displeased with ourselves and with life.

It's striking to read in Mark's Gospel that the first words the Father utters about his Son are "You are my Son, whom I love; with you I am well pleased" (Mk 1:11). Mark opens the story of Jesus' life with the words every child longs to hear from his or her parent: "I love you, I'm pleased with you."

In our society love follows worth, and worth is created by works. We are trained to earn others' pleasure, acceptance, affirmation and recognition. Our identity is formed in our accomplishments. What we do defines for us who we are, and few people feel as if they've done enough. The gospel of Jesus Christ is shocking in that it begins, rather than ends, with affirmation. "My Son, whom I love; with you I am well pleased" is heard before Jesus is recorded as having done anything!

This is the utterly liberating news of the gospel for us too. In Christ, God celebrates who we are. In Christ, God is pleased with us, not because of what we are or what we have done, but because of who he is. "This is how God showed his love among us: He sent his one and only Son into the world that we might live through him. This is love: not that we loved

God, but that he loved us. . . . Dear friends, since God so loved us, we also ought to love one another" (1 Jn 4:9-11).

Not only is God's love in Christ the example of how we are to love, but it creates the possibility of our acting in love. We love through him. This reorientation in how and why we love is the secret to a vibrant spirituality that brings eternal truth to the terrors of time, theology to earth. As we will see, it all begins in choosing where we stand.

Knowing Where to Stand

Our failure as lovers stems from our choice of the wrong place to stand. We spend most of our lives standing in loneliness and busyness, in war zones or at least demilitarized no-combat zones, in feelings of guilt and failure. The gospel shouts out to us, "Why are we wasting your time standing there?" Paul writes in Romans 5:1-2, "Therefore, since we have been justified through faith, we have peace with God through our Lord Jesus Christ, through whom we have gained access by faith into this grace in which we now stand. And we rejoice in the hope of the glory of God." What enables a life of joy-filled hopefulness rather than guilt-ridden loneliness? Standing in grace! What is grace? Peace, being at peace—the peace found in reconciled relationships.

God has reconciled us to himself in Jesus Christ. We are made acceptable because of who God is and what God has done on our behalf, not because of who we are or what we do on God's behalf.

Rather than standing in our world, with its woefully inadequate methods of justification through performance and accomplishments, class, caste and race, titles, accomplishments and acquisitions, we stand in God's grace. Tragically, most of us Christians live with one foot in grace and one in grief. Our formal theology assures us that we are justified by grace and therefore we are at peace. However, our functional theology, the one by which we live every day, mandates that we do more, give more, love more and care more. Frenzy usurps the place of peace, loneliness replaces community, and guilt drives away our awareness of grace.

I know all too well what I am describing. For years I preached a wonderful gospel of grace and lived a deadly nongospel of works. Try as hard as I might, I could never give, go, do, sacrifice or serve enough. In the grade-givers' nongospel I always pictured myself receiving a C –. Grace simply meant that God wouldn't fail me. The safety net of the cross merely brought the assurance that I couldn't flunk the Final Exam. As far as spiritual grades were concerned, I was a poor student.

This was the case until I entered for a second time what many regard as life's best classroom. Degrees in theology couldn't teach me how to live by grace. I learned it in the drama of a hospital intensive-care room. Six years after my first involuntary enrollment in the classroom of crisis—the fruit of the boating accident mentioned earlier—I once again became a bedridden student. While my body struggled with endocarditis and the doctors wondered whether I'd survive, I once again struggled with my own mortality. What if I did die? Was I ready? Had I done, given, gone enough? The answer was surely *No!* I was only thirty-two years old. I couldn't have accomplished enough to justify my life.

With the mirror of my own finitude propped dramatically before me, I could clearly see my sense of failure. But then, before my open eyes, the image changed. For no apparent reason except the intervention of the Holy Spirit, the first lines of the Shorter Catechism of the Westminster Confession came to my mind. (I'm not an impressive student of the Westminster Confession! Those are the only lines I know.) In the middle of the night, with twelve tubes penetrating my disease-saturated body, I heard, "The chief end of humankind is to glorify God and enjoy him forever."

In a flash I realized that I never would have written it that way. Surely our chief end is to glorify God by serving him forever! "Enjoy God!" What could that possibly have to do with our chief end? What God wants is our service, our sacrifice, our noble deeds done in his name!

The Journey of Grace from Our Head to Our Heart

With the word *enjoy*, grace took another step on the long journey from my head to my heart. For some of us, it's the longest path any truth must traverse. John sings of it when he writes, "If anyone acknowledges that Jesus is the Son of God, God lives in him and he in God. And so we know and rely on the love God has for us" (1 Jn 4:15-16). I may have known God's love for me in my head (my formal theology), but I relied on my efforts to make myself lovable (my functional theology—or to use current jargon, my *dysfunctional* theology). I needed to let God's love into my the theology of my everyday life.

Our freedom is found in allowing the fullness of this truth to enter our lives. It is this truth that sets "our hearts at rest in his presence" (1 Jn 3:19). This love "drives out fear, because fear has to do with punishment" (4:18).

We can love because God has first loved us. He hasn't loved us first just once. We often speak of this initiating love as something primordial, a divine covenant with creation, or as something expressed primarily in the first century in Jesus' life and death. But God loves us first every day— when we arise, when we stumble, when we soar and even when we slumber. How ungrateful we are to forget this, and to think that he has only once first loved us! When this news sinks into our lives, that in Christ the Father continually says to us these same two awesome affirmations—"You are my son or daughter whom I love, and in you I am pleased"—we are freed from all the other voices that would demand our attention and seek to define our worth by our works.

Standing in grace puts us in conflict with the dominant values of our grade-giving, status-separating societies. Thus Paul goes on to describe in Romans 5 the environment that surrounds us as we stand in grace. Surprisingly, two words sum it up: *hopeful suffering!* Grace doesn't mean the absence of conflict. In a later chapter we will explore ways in which living a life justified by grace will result in conflict. For now, suffice it to stress that we can rejoice in such conflict, for by grace "suffering produces perseverance; perseverance, character; and character, hope" (vv. 3-4). Hope is the fruit of standing in grace. When grace is our abode, we know that we are in touch with ultimate reality. The lies of the grade-givers will one day be disclosed. "And hope does not disappoint us, because God has poured out his love into our hearts by the Holy Spirit" (v. 5).

Where our hearts have been our accusers, they are transformed by grace into receptacles of God's love. Our capacity to love is not a function of our discipline or devotion. By the Holy Spirit in us, God loves others through us. Our own lovelessness, our incapacity as lovers, is no longer an ultimate obstacle. Of course we're not good lovers, but we have no excuse for remaining loveless. We can stand in grace and allow God to pour—not just place or express, but *pour*—his love out through us.

Knowing to Whom to Say Yes

It is in this context that we are prepared to hear the third affirmation that the Father spoke to his incarnate Son as recorded by Mark. After calling him the one he loves, the one in whom he is pleased, the Father called him into the wilderness so that he might face temptation and tribulation (Mk 1:12-13). He "immediately" sent the Son, his beloved Son, into the wilderness to be alone and tempted!

In our society, it's usually sons and daughters who distance themselves from their parents. They go into the far country. In fact, we have come to regard adolescent rebellion as an essential step on the path to maturation. But in the Gospel the Father *sends* the Son to the wilderness. He's sent not to earn his worth but to be delivered from all lesser sources of worth and return to the only true one—the Father's love. Standing in grace requires knowing to whom to say yes and to whom to say no.

After being immersed in the affirmation of the Father's love, Jesus was immediately confronted with lesser sources of worth. Three times he was tempted to say yes to the devil. But because he knew he was so loved, he could immediately reject the devil's offers. It is only when we have the Father's *yes* ringing in our ears that we can say no to all the other voices.

Though Mark doesn't record Satan's temptations, the other Gospels clarify their threefold nature. They are pertinent to this book's topic, for these temptations are inherent in all inappropriate efforts to ground our spirituality. Whenever people say yes to the wrong voice, they bring falsehood rather than truth to life.

A universal spiritual temptation is to use our relationship with God for our material advantage. God will reward our faithfulness with personal well-being! Godliness will surely lead to great gain! Through this ever-popular theology, the Spirit is treated as our servant, as we audaciously risk attempting to usurp the place of God in our lives.

Little needs to be said regarding the ways our lives are seduced by this voice of the Tempter. We've encumbered the beauty of our souls and transformed our hearts into busy marketplaces, endlessly preoccupied with buying and selling things. Our lives are so dominated by the innumerable times we've said yes to our things that there's little space in our soul to say yes to God. We've worshiped and served the creature and all that's created, and made the Creator our servant. Even our churches succumb to the temptation to make sure that their architecture, furnishings, decor and attire properly reflect an atmosphere of success.

Jesus said no to the tempting voice of material comfort and well-being by uttering a strong yes to his true source of strength. "It is written, 'One does not live by bread alone' " (Lk 4:4 NRSV). Jesus drowned out the enticing voice of material success, even to meet basic, legitimate needs, by asserting, "I'm more than a mere physical body, more than a manufacturer and consumer of things."

Quickly following the temptation to material well-being comes the invitation to succeed socially. "Merely worship me," the Adversary cajoles, "and all people will bow before you." Lest we hastily pass over this temptation as absurd, we must face the obvious—our society is preoccupied with the lives of the rich and famous. Thousands stand for hours in the rain, awaiting the passing of the limousine of a rock star, sports star, movie star or political star. We take tours to see their homes, spend millions on their bestselling, ghost-written autobiographies, and inevitably end the tour and close the book feeling diminished by the experience. Our faces aren't as beautiful. Our carpets and furnishings seem shabbier. Our bank accounts are more meager. No one lines up to watch *us* pass!

For several years my family and I lived near the Scottish autumn castle of Britain's royal family. Balmoral Castle is splendidly situated on the banks of the beautiful Dee River, in the center of a vast estate. We learned that when the family is in residence, for a few weeks each year, visitors can stand by the road on a Sunday morning to watch the family drive the short distance from the castle to the church for morning worship. Since

Balmoral was only a short distance from our house, we decided one rainy Sunday morning to make the pilgrimage. As we drove into the parking lot, we discovered that thousands of others had beat us to it. Guard dogs sniffed for bombs and "bobbies" controlled the crowd as we made our way to a spot in the roadside queue.

Within minutes the royal family passed by, waving royal waves to the rain-soaked throng. Everyone's clothes seemed damper, cars seemed colder, and lives seemed shabbier as they drove away. We often feel impoverished by being around kings.

"Accept my methods, for the end justifies the means," urges the Tempter, "and success shall be yours." Jesus' penetrating yes to his Father speaks a cutting no to this idolatrous worship. "It is written, 'Worship the Lord your God and serve him only' " (Lk 4:8). With this yes Jesus further brings truth to life and brings our spirituality to earth. "I desire only my Father and his favor—favor I've already received. The need to please others and receive their praise will not control or captivate me."

After the royal family had passed, my family and I didn't climb into our old Ford to drive home. For though thousands had been in the queue to watch the queen drive by, only a few were in queue to enter the church and worship the King. We had the privilege of spending an hour in worship of the King of creation, within only a few yards of the Queen of Britain, Prince Philip, Charles, Diana and the rest of the family. The prime minister and her husband happened to be there that morning too. In a shared act of worship, we all knelt before creation's Monarch.

The final temptation is more insidious than the others. It strikes at the heart of our desire both to be spiritual successes and to have our faith validated by our experience. If this temptation is misunderstood, all the themes I've been mentioning—sensory spirituality, visual theology, tangible truth—only reinforce it.

Deep within us is the desire to make God an object of our experience rather than the Subject of our experience. We want to prove our spirituality by our answered prayers, our miraculous deeds, our spiritual gifts and our experiences of God's mighty acts in our lives.

That seems all so legitimate. Surely God wants us to know and experience him! Surely God wants to do great and wonderful things in our lives! Why would saying yes to that be soul-destroying?

We flock to lectures and sermons and eagerly buy books by Christians who will show us how to have a deeper spiritual life, how to see the Spirit perform mighty signs and wonders through us. We like preachers and pastors and televangelists who exude spiritual power. Far better that than powerless preachers! So what is the issue here?

The deepest temptation of the spiritual life is to try to manipulate God for my own ends. "Do not put the Lord your God to the test," Jesus said (Lk 4:12). In order to say yes to true spirituality, Jesus must say a loud no: *Do not!* God is not our genie. Do not treat God as one who must perform for you.

Spiritual health depends on the determination never to manipulate God for our own ends. No wonder we feel spiritually diseased. Just as we fear that our lives are failing the divine test, so we constantly put God to the test to perform for us the way we think a good God should. "I study the Bible, go to church and try to be nice to others. Why did God let this [fill in the blank: life-threatening cancer, inconvenient head cold, shattering divorce, deep discouragement, etc.] happen to me?"

Years ago, the truth of this was brought home to me as I rode in a taxi in Bangkok. Like good capitalists, taxi drivers there fill their cabs as full as possible. A man from Malaysia was riding virtually on my lap as we journeyed to the airport. It was natural to fall into conversation.

"Where are you going?" I innocently asked.

"I'm going to India," was the reply.

Curious, I pursued, "Why are you going there?"

"I'm on vacation from my work in a factory in Malaysia and am going to Kerala to organize a labor union among fishermen."

"That's an unusual way to spend your vacation," I commented.

"Well, you see," he said, "I'm a Marxist, and everything I do has to do with my commitment to the revolution. It determines where I work, where I live, how I spend my money, even how I spend my vacation.

"Where are you going?" he demanded.

"I'm also going to India, to visit some Indian pastors who are friends of mine and have wonderful ministries among the poor," I replied.

"You American Christians don't stand a chance against us Marxists," was his immediate response. It wasn't too difficult to guess how he knew I was an American.

"Why?" I asked.

"Because for you, the integrating value in your life is self-interest," he asserted. "You become a Christian because you want to have your sins forgiven and be sure of going to heaven. You pray because you want God to do things for you. You go to church because you think it will make you more successful and happier and keep your family together. Everything you do, you do for yourself. But everything I do is for the revolution. I'm willing to die for the revolution. To die for self-interest is a contradiction in terms. That's why you Christians don't stand a chance against us Marxists."

While history will surely prove this man's prophecy wrong, his diagnosis of our malady strikes home. It was only when Jesus said, "Do not put the Lord your God to the test," that the devil departed from him.

Knowing When to Stop

Seeing God pour out his love in our hearts requires being set free to stand in grace. Standing in grace requires knowing to whom to say no and to whom to say yes. A battle is raging all around us in our graceless world. Are we casualties, saying yes to disgrace and no to grace? Are we running, fleeing and crushed down by the onslaught of "shoulds," "oughts" and "supposed-tos"? It is tragically easy for us to mistake motion for progress and speed for accomplishment. We are easily seduced into allowing busyness to blur the beauty of our lives, with to-do lists reigning over us as our temporal lords.

The gospel of grace confronts us with a penetrating question: Have we been so become so accustomed to living in "disgrace" that we've succumbed to the Tempter's seductive accusations and are not even aware of the conflicts that surround us? Our capacity to stand in grace is the greatest gift we can bring to the world. Saying the right yes and the right no requires knowing not only how to stand in grace and to whom to give our obedience, but also when to *stop!*

We race through life like blind sleepwalkers, certain that we're in touch with reality but actually walking in a different world. I'm well practiced in the art of sleepwalking. Each time there comes a moment, when my wife is seeking to rouse me from my enacted dream, during which I don't know whether to stop what I'm doing and heed her call to return to bed or continue my frenzied activity. Most likely I'm engaged in some urgent rescue mission, such as seeking to save a great ship from crashing into a hidden reef.

My wife gently tells me, "Come back to bed." To whom do I listen? Do I stop my somnambulatory service and return to bed? Or do I stop listening to her call and continue on my mission?

All my dreamy emotions want to drown out her call. Yet years of experience tell me that most likely she's right. If I really do need to save the ship, I can do it in the morning. In actual fact, upon awakening in the morning I've never been disappointed that I'd returned to bed rather than continued my rescue mission.

If we are going to walk in tune with the Truth, if we are going to bring truth to life and theology to earth, to whom do we listen and what do we stop doing? The wonder of the gospel is that while we were still spiritually asleep, Christ said the final no to sin, Satan, suffering and evil, and said yes to God on our behalf. Now by the Spirit, God awakens us and speaks Christ's yes and no through us.

Two dreams I've actually dreamed vividly illustrate what I mean by this. Both occurred during the time of my hospitalization with endocarditis. In neither dream were my feet in motion, for I was confined to bed. Both were so vivid that they have marked me for life.

STOP!

I was standing on the stern of a ferry as it pulled out from the dock. Rather than being filled with excitement over the adventure of the voyage, my heart filled with horror as I watched the growing gulf between me and the dock. My wife and children, my home and hopes were on the shore, and the gap between us was growing bigger and bigger. I didn't want to be on this ferry. I hadn't chosen this trip. I wasn't packed, I wasn't ready. In sheer desperation, as the distance became insurmountable, I cried out in my dream, "Stop!"

Immediately the ferry disappeared, and I awoke with my heart monitor beeping. A nurse rushed into my room to see what was wrong. Covered with sweat and panting for breath, I told her that I must have had a bad dream.

"I'm scared," I said. "I'm afraid I might die."

She said, "Most people in your situation are afraid. Want me to give you something to help you sleep?"

What skill in pastoral care! I thought. "No, I'll try to sleep on my own."

I thought about my dream. I wasn't ready to die. If I died that night, I would feel as if I had succeeded in many areas in life—my pastoral ministry, my enabling of others in missionary service, my receiving of respect from my church. But I believed that I had lived by the wrong priorities. Service dominated my life. My devotion to God was subordinated to my devotion to "God's work." My enjoyment of my wife and children and friends came after my devotion to ministry. I had been a success in areas where, in the light of death, I could afford to fail. I felt like a failure in areas where, when brought to the light of eternity, I didn't want to be a failure.

It was at that point that I heard the reminder, which I mentioned earlier, of my "chief end" as stated in the Shorter Catechism. I realized that my ferry had stopped because I still had much to learn in the school of grace. I wasn't ready to stand before the Lord.

For all of us, there will come a time that our ferry *won't* stop. What will it take for us to be able to say with Paul in Romans 5, "We have peace with God . . . and we rejoice in our hope of sharing the glory of God" (vv. 1-2 RSV)?

STAND!

I dreamed that I was fleeing through a sticky night like a frightened rabbit, desperately seeking to escape the hunters in the safety of an elusive hole. But there was no hiding place to be found. No sanctuary was available. The darkness clung to me like jungle vines. I couldn't move forward fast enough. Everything seemed to oppose me as I struggled forward. Even the ground was my foe. Ankle-deep, cementlike mud made every step a costly but insufficient success.

My adversaries knew no obstacles, for they had no feet with which to touch the ground. Lacking legs and arms, they flew through the darkness like winged black holes, sucking all life into their all-consuming emptiness. Their hideous shrieks grew closer each second. Soon I would be theirs.

Just as I was about to be engulfed by Terror, a commanding Voice arrested my flight. One word cut through the darkness: "Stand!"

I stopped and I stood.

My pursuers surged around, but as I was about to be devoured by their vacuum embrace, they became the ones who were pursued. A blazing light pierced the darkness. It raced past me like a comet hurtling through the sky. The terrifying shrieks of my adversaries changed into cries of the terrified. They scattered in panic, but escape was impossible, and their deadening darkness was absorbed by life-giving Light.

Within a few seconds—seconds that carried with them the enduring depth of eternity—their sinister shrieks were silenced. Their hideous antilife forms were absorbed by the Light that engulfed them.

I stood. This time, rather than standing in terror, I stood in awe.

As I watched, the ball of light raced on ahead of me and ascended to the top of a hill. There, to my amazement, it took the form of a cross. As the light from this luminous cross pierced the surrounding darkness, dawn broke.

This wasn't an ordinary dawn. It seemed like a cosmic dawn. I was a spectator to the dawning of God's new creation. The spreading dawn was greeted by an earthy chorus of praise as the now visible trees and flowers and hills burst forth into songs of joy. Truth had come to life.

I awoke, covered with sweat and overwhelmed with wonder. It had been *only* a dream, but a dream that rang with reality more clearly than I had experienced in all my waking moments. What did it mean?

The answer was obvious. Very little analysis was required to recognize that as I'd slept, I'd had the privilege of seeing past the veil of the visible into the heart of Life.

We stand on the frontline of the war of grace against disgrace. As God gives us the capacity to stand, simply stand in grace, we manifest his victory over all that defiles, divides and dehumanizes us. We participate in the victory of the Light of Life over the soul-destroying darkness of Death.

"This is love: not that we loved God, but that he loved us and sent his Son as an atoning sacrifice for our sins" (1 Jn 4:10). "And this is the victory that conquers the world, our faith. Who is it that conquers the world but the one who believes that Jesus is the Son of God?" (1 John 5:4-5 NRSV).

What is our faith? We stand in the grace of our Lord Jesus Christ. We stand in peace with the triune God—Father, Incarnate Son and Holy Spirit. We stand in hope, and hope will never disappoint us, for the love of God is poured out in our hearts through the Spirit. "For while we were still weak, at the right time Christ died for the ungodly. . . . For if while we were enemies, we were reconciled to God through the death of his Son, much more surely, having been reconciled, will we be saved by his life. But much more than that, we even boast in God through our Lord Jesus Christ" (Rom 5:6, 10-11 NRSV).

Truth isn't brought to life through our own efforts to "be spiritual" or to apply our best efforts to overcome our weaknesses. Truth has been brought to life—to our lives—in Jesus Christ. This is theology brought to earth. He is truth made visible.

The triune God lifts the veil that shrouds our lives, so that we can see, hear, taste, smell and feel his eternal reality in the midst of our daily lives. Several crises and dreams helped to lift the veil from my life. However, it's a continual, ongoing need. We are so easily blinded. Our hearing is quickly dulled. Our senses of taste and smell are distracted by the aromas of our world. The touches of pleasure and pain often deaden our sensibilities.

Though our five senses aren't in themselves adequate vehicles for encountering the invisible God, behind each is a spiritual sense that, when awakened, opens up for us the awareness of another world. Let's turn now to consider the great gift of our spiritual senses.

2
Awakening Our Spiritual Senses

IT IS A STRANGE TRAGEDY THAT WESTERN SPIRITUALITY AND WORSHIP ARE OFTEN held captive by a preoccupation with the human rather than the divine. Instead of awakening us to perceive the gracious presence of God, our worship services too often begin and end with ourselves: what we do, hear and experience. We evaluate worship in terms of what we get out of it, what we like, what we feel and what we receive. Sometimes our senses are merely dominated by what others are wearing, how they sound and, if their perfume was too liberally applied, even how they smell.

Sanctuaries, places of Spirit-filled communion, have been replaced by auditoriums—places of acoustically perfect listening, or even oratoriums. We worship by listening to electronically enhanced human words. Much contemporary Protestant "worship" begins with thirty minutes of hearing ourselves sing and climaxes in thirty minutes of hearing the preacher preach.

It is no surprise that many people today are flocking to worship places in which the human voice and leader are less preeminent. Liturgies, silence, symbol and ritual are being sought as places where God may be found. In our highly materialistic society, people are fleeing that which is human, and human-made, to find the spiritual. But does this mean that the human and the material are obstacles to encountering the divine and the spiritual?

Wordless Messengers

God has provided us with objective, tangible truth that integrates our subjectivity and God's objectivity, our materiality and God's spirituality. Much to our surprise, this truth that we can touch is readily available through wordless messengers. In fact, we need silence to hear the One who is the Word. As a gift to us, deafened as we are today by noise, God has provided us with wordless ways of knowing God.

T. S. Eliot once lamented, "Where shall the Word be found, where will the word / Resound? Not here, there is not enough silence."[1] The silence in which God's Word is found isn't a self-defined, interior silence in which we seek to hear God within the prison of our own subjectivity. Rather, God's embodied Word saves us from a nebulous "spirituality" rooted in our own experiences and understandings. Disembodied, uprooted "spirituality" can mean anything I want and take any forms I choose to give it. Knowing how deeply we need objective, tangible truth, God has provided us with mundane ways of touching God and being rooted in him.

The church has historically called these the *sacraments*. The sacraments are the primary form of tangible truth that God gives us today. Understanding their richness opens up to us a wealth of sensory spirituality—ways in which we can mundanely encounter the eternal God in what we eat, drink, touch, smell and hear.

To understand the rich objectivity of these wordless messengers, it is helpful to explore briefly their history. Literally, the word *sacrament* means sacred oath *(sacra mentum)*. It referred to the oath of loyalty that a Roman soldier took to the divine Caesar. This sacred oath distinguished

a member of the army from a civilian. Interestingly, the word for one
had not taken the sacrament (a civilian) was *paganus,* a pagan. As I
mentioned in the previous chapter, at my first encounter with the Lord's
Supper I indeed felt like a civilian. I felt like an outsider at someone else's
dinner party. In the Roman world, you were a soldier, a citizen or a pagan.
I recognized that from this point of view I was a pagan, and my hunger
was stimulated for more.

The *sacramentum* was a public pledge of ultimate loyalty. Through this
vow the soldier promised to have no other allegiances, no higher loyalties.
It was an outward and visible pledge of an internal and total loyalty. For
this reason, the early church decided that it could not allow enlisted
soldiers to be baptized and receive the Lord's Supper. Soldiers had already
taken a sacrament—pledged ultimate loyalty to Caesar. They had said that
they had no higher loyalty than to the divine emperor; yet for Christians,
Christ must supersede everything and everyone else.

In adopting this word for its central celebrations, the church proclaimed that in coming to Christ one enlisted as a full-time servant of
Christ. There could be no higher loyalty. One had taken a sacrament to
the Divine Christ. Similarly, it is no surprise that the church adopted the
word *pagan* to refer to those who were not enlisted in Christ's service.
You were either a Christian or a pagan.

Augustine gave the church the definition which has formed the classic
foundation for a Christian understanding of the sacraments: the sacraments are an outward and visible sign of the inward and spiritual grace
we have received in Jesus Christ, by which we are adopted into relationship with God.[2] These ordinary, visible forms become tangible expressions
of an extraordinary, invisible encounter.

The sacraments are visible words. Through these words that we can
touch, we hear the voice and encounter the Spirit of God.[3] Thus when
I speak of them as wordless messengers, I am not opening the door to
a totally nebulous, self-defined spirituality. The messengers may be without words, but they are not silent. We don't determine what they mean,
what they are saying. We don't define them. Rather, they are filled with
divine content. In a very real sense *they* define *us.*

Knowing how utterly physical we are, God does indeed want us to taste and see his goodness (Ps 34:8). We need not deny or suppress our human, physical, material, corporeal existence in order to encounter the divine, spiritual, immaterial, infinite God: the wonder of the Christian faith is that the physical can actually be a vehicle for encountering the spiritual. An outward and visible sign of an inward and spiritual grace!

Our sophisticated palates are prone to find such ordinary food unpalatable. We tend toward the belief that God can be known only in esoteric, rarefied ways, requiring the guidance of spiritual gourmets who have mastered extraordinary disciplines. In contrast, biblical faith indicates that God has usually chosen for his goodness and truth to be known in ordinary, material ways: a garden for Adam and Eve, a rainbow for Noah, some "what is it?"—manna—for desert pilgrims. It is no wonder that Jesus repeatedly depicted our ultimate goal as a banquet in the kingdom of God.

We are called to sit at table with God, where he is simultaneously the host and provider, our companion at the table and the meal itself. The mystery of this is unavoidable. We prefer to confine God to abstract forms—a force, a power, a source, an Ideal, an Idea. God prefers to join us at a table.

After years as a pastor, one day I was meeting with two very gifted women in my church, trying to understand why I was so addicted to my own accomplishments, unwilling to accept that God accepted me without regard to my performance. I could preach and teach a wonderful doctrine of justification by grace, but I nullified it in my actions by a frenetic, harried, heart-threatening ungospel of justification through works. I lived as if my existence were justified by what I did.

These saintly women led me in prayer, and there I encountered a vision of Jesus in my primary school. I was a young boy standing in the hallway. At the sound of the noon bell all my friends had fled class for the lunchroom, leaving me alone and lonely. No one wanted to play with me.

Up walked Jesus in a striped polo shirt, carrying a sack lunch just like mine. To my utter amazement he looked me in the eye—I still remember that gaze—and said, "Tim, let's go outside under that tree and eat our lunch together."

In that simple envisioned encounter I broke into tears, and my life broke open to new dimensions of theological understanding. The Lord of the universe was not merely a cosmic Teacher always trying to get me to grow. He was not merely the ultimate CEO, relentlessly assigning new tasks for me to perform. He wanted to eat lunch with me! He simply enjoyed being with me.

My theology of grace moved as it never had before from my head to my heart. Like Nicodemus of old, I was forever changed by Jesus' words, "Let's eat together."

On the canvases of water, bread and wine, God has painted a picture of his promises and sets it continually before our eyes. They become for us pillars of our faith, built on the foundation of the utterly reliable Word of God. In them we can hear and receive the riches of God's grace and goodness which He lavishes upon us.

I do not suggest that the sacraments contain life or grace in themselves (although this view is held in some churches). Rather, the sacraments point us to Christ, who is Life. Their value depends totally on the presence of the Spirit of God. They are not magical elements with their own intrinsic value.

This is an essential reminder in our sensual, experience-saturated society, where our eyes are easily diverted to focus on the power of outward forms and experiences. In polar opposition to one contemporary trend to flee the material in pursuit of the spiritual, we find another trend in the "New Age" effort totally to mingle them. Our postsecular culture is laden with the animist belief of traditional societies, which asserts that material things are supercharged with spiritual power, *mana*. Misunderstood, the sacraments can easily be dumped into the popular spiritually eclectic shopping basket that contains crystals, tarot cards, Gregorian (or possibly Tibetan) chants, incense, drums and a guru or two. Many people collect this "spiritual stuff" to expand their encounter with the divine.

A little bite of bread and a sip of grape juice! What could these have to do with the holy, infinite, invisible God? Possibly if they were served in a silver tray and chalice, but surely not from a paper plate and cup!

Much to our surprise, the Spirit of God moves through simple signs, leading us to the profound reality they signify. God meets us in Jesus Christ, cleanses us from our sin and draws us into relationship with himself. God wants to eat with us! To understand this, and to clarify its radical distinction from today's animistic pantheism, which seeks the divine presence surrounding us in all material things, it is important to explore the relationship of the sacraments to Jesus Christ.

Jesus Christ: God's Life Made Visible

The Incarnate Son himself is *the* true sacrament, in whom the others find their meaning and significance. He himself is the outward and visible sign of an inner and spiritual grace. In him the grace of the eternal God comes to us in mortal humanity. As John says, "No one has ever seen God, but his only begotten Son, Jesus Christ, is the explanation of God" (my paraphrase—see Jn 1:18). Christ is the *explanation* of God, full of grace and truth! God is explained not in the form of words and concepts, but in the form of flesh and bone: the Word conceived, the Incarnate Son.

Instead of the universal human religious pursuit of God and simultaneous flight from him, God himself has come in pursuit of fleeing humankind. Furthermore, rather than God giving a demand and then waiting for humankind's response, in the Incarnate Son God offers a perfect response to his own demand. Brunner describes this as the "great inversion of existence":

> For in its actual specific message the Bible does not deal with the God who demands and the man who acts, like every other sacred book; but it speaks of the God who acts and the man who receives the Divine gift. This is the great inversion of existence. Previously, life, even at its best, is always a life directed towards God; now, henceforth life is lived from God as its center. In this new possibility of life the old life is seen to be perverted, and it becomes manifest that the attempt to attain God by our own efforts rather than to base all our life on God, ˹ˑˈˢˑˈalism, is the root of sin.[4]

Jesus Christ: Our Life Made Spiritual

Jesus is God's response to us, and also our response to God. Our own relationship with God is possible and present in Christ. Like a mighty symphony of praise, there are three movements to this sacrament of incarnate grace.

In Jesus Christ the seeking, gracious God comes in pursuit of his fleeing human creatures. The Son has come to seek and to save that which is lost. God takes the initiative in finding us. He has not waited for us to find him.

But it was not enough for God merely to find us. In our tortured desire for independence from God, we are not always willing to be found. We seek and flee at the same time. Thus to save his human creatures, God offered in Jesus Christ the perfect human response that we in ourselves are unable and unwilling to make. He is both the sacrament and the reception of the sacrament! He receives the grace of God in our flesh, in our name, in our place. As the Catholic theologian Edward Schillebeeckx affirms,

> Jesus is not only the revelation of the redeeming God; he is also the supreme worshiper of the Father, the supreme realization of all religion. . . . Whatever Christ does as a free man is not only a realization in human form of God's activity for our salvation; it is also at the same time the positive human acceptance, representative for all of us, of this redeeming offer from God.[5]

Paul shouts out this truth in a mighty chorus of praise found in 2 Corinthians 5:17-18: "Therefore, if anyone is in Christ, he is a new creation; the old has gone, the new has come! All this is from God, who reconciled us to himself through Christ." As the divine/man, Christ is our reconciliation with the Father. The intimate communion between the Father, Son and Spirit has become physical and material, incarnate in the stuff of God's creation.

The focus has radically shifted. No longer is our religious gaze fixed on the adequacy or inadequacy of what we do for God. Rather, we are liberated to celebrate and participate in what God has done on our behalf. Schillebeeckx comments, "Because the saving acts of the man Jesus are performed by a divine person, they have a divine power to save, but because this divine power to save appears to us in visible form, the saving activity of Jesus is *sacramental*. . . . The man Jesus, as the personal visible realization of the divine grace of redemption, is *the* sacrament."[6]

Yet we must participate, and so we come to the third movement of grace. By the action of the Spirit of God, we share in the Son's relationship with the Father. The Spirit adopts us, freeing us to address God as Father, Abba. We become by grace what the Son is by nature—sons and daughters of God. The "great inversion" leads to the *magnificent exchange:* "Christ took what was ours that he might give us what was his: he takes our broken humanity and cleanses it by his self-sanctifying life of obedience. Now in the Spirit he gives us back our humanity cleansed and redeemed: take, eat, this is broken for you."[7]

This is why Christ proclaimed that it was better for us that he leave, that he no longer be physically present (Jn 16:7). That which was confined to space and time in his incarnate flesh can now be universally present as he makes himself present through the Spirit in his body, the church. In him the church itself becomes an expression of the sacrament of Christ, an outward and visible sign of an inward and spiritual grace: the body of Christ on earth!

Material Spirituality

If it is as a human being that the Incarnate Son embodies God's grace, then our creatureliness is no longer an obstacle for our encounter with the infinite, invisible God. Finite creatures and the infinite Creator can actually commune. God has shown us his face in a human body. Creaturely forms can continue to convey to us the grace of God without asserting that everything creaturely is itself divine.

This is shockingly, indeed scandalously unique among the world's religions. In Islam the ultimate sin is to identify Allah with anything material. The Creator and creation exist in total distinction. In Hinduism and Buddhism they exist in total identification; in fact, ultimate release comes only when we are delivered from the illusion of separate, material existence. In contrast, the gospel asserts that in Christ the spiritual God, though radically different from his creation, has made himself perfectly available in material flesh.

The sacraments therefore continue this wondrous mystery of God's presence in Christ in ongoing earthly forms. Bread, water and wine express to us the triune God's perfect response on our behalf to himself in Christ's obedient baptism and in his loving self-offering on the cross. As James Torrance says, "Christ's baptism is our baptism, set forth in our water baptism; Christ's sacrifice is our sacrifice, set forth at the table; Christ's worship is our worship, set forth in our worship and prayers."[8]

Such incarnate grace draws forth from us a joyous shout of praise and thanksgiving. "Here lies the mystery, the wonder, the glory of the Gospel, that He who is God, the Creator of all things, and worthy of the worship and praises of all creation, should become man and *as a man worship God*, and as a man lead us in our worship of God, that we might become the sons [and daughters] of God we are meant to be."[9]

The tedium of human-centered religiosity, wherein we constantly wonder if we've given, done, loved, prayed, worshiped, experienced, sacrificed enough is ended in Christ's crucified shout: *"It is finished!"* Enough has been done! That which needed to be done has been done in such a way that it needs never be done again. Humankind is reconciled to God.

I'm sure all this was told to me many times before I was gripped by its liberating implications. But somehow, tragically, the full extent of the life-giving liberty of this eluded me for the first twenty years of my Christian faith. I had never fully heard of the great inversion and the magnificent exchange. I relentlessly graded myself on the quality of my response to God. I usually only barely gave myself a passing mark. I felt as if I was never doing enough and assumed that God thought likewise.

Although my prayerful vision of Jesus with a sack lunch wanting to eat with me opened a new window through which I looked with wonder at God, I still was not fully free to sit with him under that tree. There were too many things I needed to do for him before I dared be so audacious as to sit down with him. Like the Martha in all of us, I busied myself in fruitful, at times fretful and occasionally fearful service of God.

The gift of my eventual exhaustion propelled me to a sabbatical in

Scotland, during which I had no more strength to serve. I could no longer worry about how many points I had on the Great Spiritual Scoreboard. Instead, through my studies and through a marvelous community of Christians who accepted me simply as a fellow pilgrim, I found grace more deeply than ever before. The magnificent exchange!

By grace God gives us what He demands. *He draws near to us to give Himself to us in wonderful love and communion, in an act where He draws us near to Himself* in Christ. . . . When Christ assumed our humanity, for our sakes consecrated Himself, in our name suffered, died, rose again, ascended to the Father, *we* suffered, died, rose again, ascended to the Father *in Him*. . . . Because Jesus has assumed our name, confessed our sins, died our death, risen and ascended in our humanity to intercede for us, God has accepted us in Him.[10]

Finally I found the freedom to join Jesus with his lunch sack under that tree.

Spiritual Materiality

There's more. In Christ, the Sacrament of grace, not only do we find the materiality of the spiritual, but we also discover the spirituality of the material. The Enlightenment convinced many that the invisible God could not be fully known in visible form or by finite minds. As a result, Protestant sacraments became mere memorials—pious memory exercises. Through these memorials human beings were reminded of what the Divine has done so as to inspire our strenuous moral effort and our fleeting conformity to Christ's example. The focus shifted back to us. Rather than celebrating what God has done, is doing and will do for, in and through us, we were reminded of our responsibility to act for God. The duty was ours.

Duty is fine and can elicit some formidably wonderful responses, but left to itself it soon becomes deadly. As C. S. Lewis says, "Duty is the cast put around broken love." At times we must have duty as a temporary aid until our love heals. But if we were permanently encased by duty, we would perish rather than thrive.

No wonder in our own era many spiritually fatigued people, tired out by a human-centered religiosity and yet still in an unsatisfied pursuit of the sacred, have avoided the church and run into the waiting arms of Hinduism in the guise of the New Age movement. There they can find release from their pursuit of God in the assertion that they need look no further than themselves. They are, in fact, divine.

The gospel and a Christ-centered view of the sacraments steer us through a middle course. We need say neither that the spiritual is inaccessible to the material nor that the material is in itself spiritual. Rather, spirituality and materiality perfectly and uniquely meet in the Incarnate Son.

Jesus invites us to eat with him, but—dare we say it?—the sack lunch itself becomes him. He is the Bread of Life come to our world. We eat his flesh and drink his blood. If the words recorded in John 6 were not his own, any culture with a taboo on cannibalism might find this image repulsive. Common ordinary foodstuffs, a bite of bread and a taste of grape juice, become for us the incarnate body of the Son of God.

Jesus Christ: God's Love Made Physical

One of the early church fathers, Irenaeus, loved to proclaim that the Son and the Spirit are the two arms of the Father by which he embraces the world. In the sacraments we can experience this embrace. They make God's love something we can touch and taste. In our word-weary, sensory-specific world, God knows that we need to touch and be touched by love if we are to know it. Dare we say, we need to touch and be touched by God if we are to know him. Therefore, in an elaboration of Augustine's definition, the sacraments can be understood as *the physical expression of the gift of the love of God in our dying and our rising on earth together in Christ.* This working definition will guide us through all this book's subsequent exploration of "sensory spirituality."

Baptism and the Eucharist root our spirituality in its proper source. We don't find "the Spiritual," or "god," within ourselves. We don't initiate the search for God. We don't even make ourselves acceptable to God or more spiritual for God. Our spirituality is God's gift. He comes to us. `` initiated and indeed established our relationship in Christ.

In this way Christian faith is unlike every other religion: our devotion doesn't begin with what we offer, an offering we provide. It begins with God's offering of himself to us. Ours is in essence a passive reception of God's gift. All we can do is receive—receive the water, receive the bread and receive the wine.

The sacraments make this vividly clear. A mystery! God makes his seemingly inaccessible, infinite life present to us in ways we can taste and touch. No wonder Calvin said, "I shall not be ashamed to confess that it is a secret too lofty for either my mind to comprehend or my words to declare. And to speak more plainly, I rather experience than understand it."[11]

In a world that constantly challenges us to doubt God's goodness and question whether he is indeed a faithful Lord, the sacraments seal to us the reality of his presence and the promise of his sovereign triumph. To quote Calvin again: "Sacraments are physical exercises which make us more certain of the trustworthiness of God's Word. And because we are of the flesh, they are shown us under things of flesh, to instruct us according to our dull capacity, and to lead us by the hand as tutors lead children."[12]

My wife and I woke early one morning in Kathmandu to the sound of bells ringing throughout this holy city. These weren't the giant gongs of church bells, nor were they the tranquil tinkle of cow or sheep bells. Rather, they were the gentle, rhythmic peal of hand-held bells, as Hindu devotees prepared their morning *puja*.

Looking out the window, I saw dozens of women walking though the dark street to their temples. Baskets carefully balanced on their heads carried offerings of flowers, incense, rice and fruit. They had sacrificed sleep to waken and feed their deities, preparing their gods and themselves for the day.

In contrast, God in Christ sacrificed his life to awaken us. The sacraments ring out the shocking news that God has offered his own sacrifice and devotion on our behalf. The bells of the gospel summon us to come to the water, to the feast, to come and eat (Is 55).

Lest this sounds too simple, we must be reminded of what we receive when we receive these gifts of God's love. We receive our own death: the death of our effort to define and form our lives independently from God. In taking these sacraments, we swear our sole and ultimate loyalty to the divine Lord. We don't merely add something else to our lives, placing loyalty to Christ alongside all our other loyalties. We acknowledge a radical disruption of our life and the reorientation of our allegiances. We have only one master, one commander-in-chief, one CEO. As Brunner says, "Henceforward our whole attitude towards the world and towards humanity is completely altered. . . . Through faith we have become volunteers in the Divine army."[13]

In many parts of the world baptism has degenerated into christening, a name-giving ceremony. All loving parents want to have their child "done." Baptism is regarded as a socially required rite of passage, celebrating a child's entrance into the world. The spiritual significance of the event is often buried under social custom. Often the baptized infant doesn't reappear at the church door until his or her wedding day. Thus in Scotland people often refer to Christianity as a "four-wheeled religion," with the wheels of the baby pram on the way to baptism, the limousine departing from a wedding, the hearse on the way to the grave.

If we really grasped the wonder (and even the horror) of what baptism represents, we wouldn't regard it with as much social sweetness. Once I was baptizing a most reluctant infant, who burst into tears as the water dribbled onto her forehead. The parents cringed in embarrassment, and the congregation shifted awkwardly in their seats. But it suddenly occurred to me: maybe this baby was one of the few people present who really understood what was happening! I commented to the congregation, "Dying to oneself is never easy. We seldom let go of ourselves without tears."

But the gifts of grace are not all dour and harsh. They are the gift of cleansing, healing and new life. Paul writes in Romans 6:4-8,

> Therefore we have been buried with him by baptism into death, so that, just as Christ was raised from the dead by the glory of the Father, so we too might walk in newness of life. . . . We know that our old self was crucified with him so that the body of sin might be destroyed, and

we might no longer be enslaved to sin. . . . But if we have died with Christ, we believe that we will also live with him.

Thus that which the sacraments celebrate gives us a new capacity to live. Paul continues by saying, "Therefore, do not let sin exercise dominion in your mortal bodies, to make you obey their passions. No longer present your members to sin as instruments of wickedness, but present yourselves to God as those who have been brought from death to life, and present your members to God as instruments of righteousness" (6:12-13). We are no longer the toys or puppets of earth's powers, easily persuaded by propaganda pressuring us to conform and succumb.

One of the most moving baptisms I ever observed was of a blind eighty-year-old, a former high-caste Hindu, who was led by his granddaughter into a pond on the outskirts of his village. He boldly confessed his faith in Christ, and as the pastor lowered him into the water, he left behind all the prestige, status and class he had possessed as a respected member of Hindu society. I'll never forget the look in his blind eyes as he rose from the water. Radiant delight flooded from his dripping face. He knew the embrace of everlasting divine love!

Sadly, in many of our Western Protestant churches we have turned baptism (and the Lord's Supper) into assembly-line rituals. We move through them as rapidly as possible, so as not to diminish the time available for the sermon. I know of many pastoral staffs who have carefully timed the distribution of the elements in order to save every second possible. We race through this opportunity to be touched by eternity, not even aware of what we've missed.

Upon someone's death, we devote an entire hour to their memorial service, reflecting on their life, mourning their death and celebrating their resurrection. We usually conclude with a reception so as to offer condolences to the family. Shouldn't we do the same when we celebrate someone's baptism and when we partake of Christ's sacrifice? Spiritual death and resurrection are actually more life-determinative than our physical death!

Through these tangible, touchable truths, eternity is brought into time. The sacraments are physical, outward, visible, touchable and tastable meeting points between the spiritual, invisible God and the material world. Spiritual truth isn't merely an idea, something mental. It isn't merely personal, purely subjective. It isn't merely something material, *mana*-infested "sacred stuff." Nor is it merely future, something for which we wait. It is very earthy, very worldly, very temporal.

As we are adopted into the Incarnate Christ, we become citizens in Christ's kingdom. New awareness, new loyalties and new life are opened up to us. Lewis Smedes comments, "Being in Christ is not only the fundamental fact of the individual Christian's existence, it is the whole new reality. It is not a side issue of Christian life. It is the new life."[14]

Thus the sacraments whet our appetite. They stimulate our senses. We discover that there's much more to life than we had previously thought. Life is much deeper, more solid and secure than we'd previously realized. As Luther said, "I am baptized and through my baptism God, who cannot lie, has bound himself in a covenant with me. . . . There is no greater comfort on earth than baptism."[15]

Yet this comfort calls us to action. One of the early church fathers, Ignatius, proclaimed that the sacraments were to be the Christian's arms. In this case, by "arms" he meant *weapons!* Just before being led to his martyrdom in Rome in the second century, he wrote to Polycarp, "Let none of you prove a deserter. Let your baptism be your arms."[16] Rather than being signs of social conformity, having one's child "done," the sacraments are in fact highly political signs of nonconformity to the established allegiances. Justin, before his martyrdom, proclaimed to the Roman Senate in A.D. 150 that the sacraments are the Christian's oath of loyalty, similar to that taken by Roman soldiers. In the third century Origen referred to baptism as a military oath, *sacramentum militiae,* and to Christians as soldiers of Christ, *milites Christi.* Tertullian understood military language clearly, for he was the son of an officer stationed in the Roman fort at Carthage. Yet in the third century he treasonously proclaimed that Christ was the Emperor, *imperator.*

Together in Christ

The church has always insisted that except in unusual circumstances, baptism and the Eucharist should be celebrated in public. They are corporate, incorporating events. They are social and not merely individual. Our encounter with the spiritual isn't merely personal, private and subjective. It is a great corporate celebration. All who are baptized are one body (I Cor 12:12-13). Wealthy and poor are equally enriched. Noble and outcast are equally humbled. As Cyprian asserted, in the sacraments we affirm that

> the church is one, which is spread abroad far and wide into a multitude by an increase of fruitfulness. As there are many rays of the sun but one light, and many branches of a tree but one strong trunk grounded in its tenacious root, and since from one spring flow many streams, although a goodly number seem outpoured from their bounty and superabundance, still, at the source unity abides. Take a ray from the body of the sun; its unity undergoes no division. Break a branch from a tree; the severed branch cannot sprout. Cut off a stream from its source; cut off, it dries up. So also the church, bathed in the light of the Lord, extends over the whole earth: yet there is one light diffused everywhere.[17]

Schisms, heresies and lifelessness come when we focus on our experience of the light, the stream or the fruit rather than on the sun, the source and the tree.

A sacred meal is the center of Christian worship. Meals are always most enjoyable when they are shared with others. Few like to dine alone. Christian worship at the Lord's Table is a feast of fellowship and community. Wolfhart Pannenberg notes that "the rediscovery of the Eucharist may prove to be the most important event in Christian spirituality in our time."[18]

It is striking that the Greek word for fellowship, *koinōnia,* is frequently used in the New Testament in reference to the Eucharist. Paul proclaims in 1 Corinthians 10:16-17 that the cup is the sharing *(koinōnia)* in the blood of Christ, and the broken bread is the sharing *(koinōnia)* in the body of Christ, for there is one loaf, one body. Thus these material ex-
ions of the divine love overcome our community-destroying individ-
n. They establish community while preserving individuality. We

don't each have our own private, self-discovered truth. We are found by the One Truth. However, our unity is very different from the political and peer-group totalitarianisms that create community only by mandating total uniformity: we don't have to surrender our individuality to find our corporate identity in Christ.

Our fractured society, which seems to find a semblance of unity only through forceful rule imposed by either "political correctness" or weapons, yearns for the discovery of a true community that overcomes divisions of race, sex, age and class. That community is found in a sacrifice of ourselves within the sacrifice of Christ. As Augustine says, "This is the sacrifice of Christians; we being many, are one body in Christ. . . . The Church herself is offered in the offering she makes to God."[19]

Clearly, the full flowering of this unity is something that we eagerly anticipate. It is not yet a fully present, fully visible reality. Thus when the church is invited to the Lord's Table, the very invitation reminds us of that which is yet to come, for we are exhorted to do this until Christ comes again (1 Cor 11:26). As a second-century church instruction manual for new believers said, "As this piece of bread was scattered over the hills and then was brought together and made one, so let your Church be brought together from the ends of the earth into your Kingdom."[20]

The fact that unity is yet to come doesn't exempt us from pursuing it in the present. Calvin comments, "For what sharper goal could there be to arouse mutual love among us than when Christ, giving himself to us, not only invites us by his own example to pledge and give ourselves to one another, but inasmuch as he makes himself common to all, also makes all of us one in himself."[21] It is tragic that at the point where Christians should most clearly find their unity, we are deeply divided. Denominations often don't recognize each other's baptisms; Christians of varying traditions exclude one another from the Lord's Table.

One final comment needs to be made about the corporate significance of the sacraments. In most church traditions, the administration of baptism and the Eucharist is reserved as the prerogative solely of the clergy. In fact, this often is the only clear distinction between ordained clergy and laypersons. But while there is a strong biblical case for the specialized role of clergy, baptism is the ordination of the laity! All Christians are ordained to full-time Christian service. The descent of the Spirit into those who are baptized turns them from civilians to soldiers. We must remember the origin of the word *sacrament*, for in baptism all Christians are commissioned soldiers. Laypersons are not Christians who serve Christ only in their spare time, as volunteers. They are full-time soldiers in the King's army, at the frontline!

If a distinction is to be made, the clergy are simply cooks and supply soldiers in this army, not generals. Jesus' command to his first disciples was to feed his sheep and tend his lambs. Clergy are called to nourish the church and help the church find the equipment it needs to stand for Christ and grow to full, united maturity in him. As Tertullian said, "On the basis of this *sacramentum* I am a soldier and am being challenged by the enemies . . . ; defending my oath I fight, am wounded, knocked down and killed. This destiny has been assigned to the soldier by the one who has taken him for duty by such a *sacramentum.*"

In the sacraments we remember all this. We are reminded of it (*anamnēsis*: Jn 16:4; 1 Cor 11:24-25). This is not simply remembering in the sense of recollection of some remote event in history. Rather, it is remembering in the Hebrew sense: participating in a past event such that we see our present life and future destiny are bound up with it. *Our* baptism is our adopted participation in *his* baptism. *Our* communion is our adopted participation in *his* body given for all. In this sense to remember is to re-*member*, to be reconnected. Once again we are made a member of that which occurred in the past. We participate in it again. Furthermore, when we re-member, we bring the past into the present. The sacraments are not a remembering of an absent, ancient Christ: they are *communion*—that which "makes common" and one.

Tragically, the church's debates over Communion and baptism have often focused on the *what* question rather than the *who* question. Rather than letting the sacraments—visible theology—prompt us to seek to understand more fully who is this Jesus Christ inwardly and spiritually ʼsent in these outward and visible signs, the church has debated over t happens to the bread and the water. We've focused on the substance of the outward sign instead of the inner presence. Debates have raged and churches have divided over questions like these: Is this literally his physical body? If so, when does it become so? Is this water really holy? How much is necessary for adequate baptism—a few drops of water? a pitcher full? a whole pool full?

As a result, the sacraments as theological teachers have often been replaced by the sacraments as systems of church control. "Had Protestant theologians been more concerned to ask the Who-question there may have been a much greater common understanding of what we mean by the eucharistic sacrifice. Who is the Christ whom we set forth in the act of anamnesis, and who is so truly present and on whose humanity we feed?"[22] We need the Spirit of God, the One whom Jesus promised as our Teacher, leading us into all truth, to do just that. We need the Spirit to enliven our celebrations of the sacraments, delivering them from routine and ritual and transforming them into life-giving encounters with the Redeemer who is present in our midst.

Tasting and touching God's presence in water, bread and wine enliven our perceptions and awaken our senses. God isn't encountered only through a withdrawal from the physical into the "spiritual" or mental. That which we taste, touch, see, hear and even smell can begin to take on sacramental dimensions.

3
Seeing God's Voice: The Mundane Encounter with Grace

IN SPITE OF ALL WE'VE SEEN ABOUT THE INCARNATION AS THE KEY TO A SPIRITUAL life that is rooted in tangible truth, the *limitations* of our five senses as tools for perceiving spiritual truth are actually most vividly revealed in the Incarnation. When Jesus was on earth, some people saw and heard God in him, but others mocked and denied. "Let those with ears hear!" Jesus said. Our inability to hear and see led us to kill Truth Incarnate. We couldn't handle truth that could be touched. Surely it wasn't Truth if it looked and sounded so much like us!

Yet as we've seen, it is precisely the incarnation event that distinguishes Christian spirituality from all other forms of human spirituality. Our spirituality does not require us to strive to escape into some ideal realm uncontaminated by evil and sin. Christian spirituality is historical—within time—and mundane—within this world; for it is rooted in the Incarnation of the Son of God in the man Jesus of Nazareth. God doesn't shrink from uniting himself to our humanity. God has actually become part of his broken, fallen creation while remaining perfect and divine. In Christ, the Son of God has taken our flesh and lived it perfectly on our behalf.

As a result, we find God within our broken, fallen lives and world. In Christ we find meaning and hope in the mundane moments of our lives. Hope is not found in escape to supposedly better circumstances or to a long-awaited better world. Hope is not found through suppressing or denying our bodies or our humanness.

Nor is hope found in a claim that we ourselves are divine. In asserting that God has identified himself with his creation, and even with us—his human creation—many today are quick to conclude that therefore *we* must be divine. Actually, if we were indeed divine, that fact would provide little comfort or assurance. What strange, impotent, easily manipulated and highly manipulative deities we would be!

Biblical hope does not depend on seeking an escape from this world, or on imagining that the world and our lives aren't broken. Our hope is found in the context of our broken flesh, in our turbulent time and in our weary world as through the Spirit we are adopted into the perfect humanity of Jesus Christ.

The Neglect of Incarnational Spirituality

Our failure to root all our theology and life in the Incarnation makes our Christian living tedious and our spiritual life vacuous. When we lack an appreciation of the significance of Christ's life, death and resurrection, the Christian life can become oppressive and wearisome. We are inundated with constant confrontations with our own needs, as well as the needs of the world. The problems that surround us seem oppressively vast, and our own resources seem tragically insufficient.

P. T. Forsyth provides a helpful reminder of the determinative significance of all that God has accomplished in Christ. "I sink under what has to be done for the world, till I realize that it is all less than what has been done. . . . The world's awful need is less than Christ's awesome victory."[1] Because of Christ's victory, the focus of the Christian faith is not on what we must do but on what has already been done on our behalf in Christ. "The weakness of much current work and preaching is that it betrays more of a sense of what has yet to be done than of what has already been done."[2]

To the extent that the Christian church has lost an incarnational spirituality, it is a very difficult place to be spiritual. Christians often feel spiritually resourceless in their confrontation with an onslaught of complex problems and mundane moments. We try to manipulate and maneuver ourselves into a "spiritual mood" or into a more meaningful life. Rather than turning to the Incarnate Son's life within the Triune God *as* our spiritual life, we seek our "own personal spiritual life" through self-help programs and worship of our own efforts.

One winter morning a three-year-old friend of ours burst out the front door and was about to run onto an ice-covered sidewalk. Reaching her before she slipped, her father called out, "Take my hand!"

She looked up at him with utter confidence and, with both her hands gripping her jacket tightly, said, "That's OK, Daddy—I don't need any help. I'm holding on to myself real tight."

In Christ, God has gripped our slippery, sinful lives and drawn us into the fullness of the triune communion. Sadly, we're all too hesitant to grab his hand.

In fact, many Christians seem to be afraid of drawing near to the Incarnate God as their spiritual life. This seems to entail major loss of control. We want a spirituality that is rooted in *our* experience rather than his. We want a relationship with God that is based on what *we* do, rather than on what he has done on our behalf. We risk contracting the soul-destroying disease of spiritual anorexia. We want to control our own lives, even if it means destroying ourselves.

Worse yet, today some spiritually anorexic churches are being led down the path of slow starvation by pastors who are overwhelmed by the complexity of the expectations placed upon them as managers, motivators and mini-messiahs. Consumed by the escalating demands of parish leadership, pastors are often afraid or unwilling to take the time required to be nourished in private prayer and Bible study. If such activities produce no immediate obvious benefit for church programs, there seems to be no time for them. Eugene Peterson's call for pastors to become contemplative (in his book *Contemplative Pastors*) sounds wonderfully life-giving but seems utterly inaccessible for a generation of clergy who feel at times that their primary contemplative materials are Day-Timers and financial spreadsheets. Unless there are radical changes, today's hungry church will be led in the future by a generation of theological students who entered seminary seeking spiritual direction and inner healing and left feeling frustrated, confused and weary.

A child who suffers from severe malnutrition, kwashiorkor, mercifully loses all appetite. After weeks of nothing to eat, the desire for food finally shuts down. When aid workers begin to dip a sugar-sweetened finger in such a child's mouth, tears are the first sign of hope. The cries of hunger mark the return of the child's appetite and the birth of hope.

The gospel of God's grace awakens our hunger. The Holy Spirit births in us the sweet reassurance that in Christ we are God's beloved sons and daughters in whom God is pleased. We cry in pain over our malnutrition and seek true food. At such a moment rehydration fluids and carefully prepared nourishment are essential. Filling the belly of a starving child with the wrong food only ensures his or her starvation.

Nourishment for an Anorexic Church

Our hungry church needs true food. If we seek only with our five senses and do not allow the Spirit to open those senses to their spiritual counterparts, we will continue in our malnutrition.

We read in Hebrews that "faith is the assurance of things hoped for, the conviction of things not seen. . . . By faith we understand that the worlds were prepared by the word of God, so that what is seen was made from things that are not visible" (Heb 11:1-3 NRSV). The gospel reverses our natural way of knowing. Through our natural senses we normally form conclusions about what we *don't* see based on an analysis of what we *do* see. This is good scientific reasoning. However, as God awakens our spiritual senses, we are enabled to form conclusions about what we *do* see based on an encounter with what we *don't* see.

This spiritual sensory awakening isn't dependent on our own efforts. God has provided the stimulus in the Incarnation. Christ makes known, explains in himself and brings to the world of our five senses the unseen God. By his work and through his Spirit, our spiritual senses are awakened to make the most mundane moments of life places of encounter with the Living God. Thus instead of finding God only as we detach ourselves from mundane demands, whether the demands of the parish or of the marketplace, with spiritually awakened senses we can make every moment an altar of communion.

Human spiritual life always involves the use of our bodies. We have no other tools or instruments in the spiritual life than them. As Dallas Willard says, "It is precisely this appropriate recognition of the body and its implications for theology that is missing in currently dominant views of Christian salvation and deliverance."[3] He goes on to say, "To withhold our bodies from religion is to exclude religion from our lives. . . . Spirituality . . . is a relationship of our embodied selves to God that has the natural and irrepressible effect of making us alive to the Kingdom of God—here and now in the material world."[4] So it is appropriate that we learn about growth in Christ by focusing on cultivating our five senses as vehicles for encountering and worshiping God.

Seeing Truth: The Gift of Spiritual Sight

God wants to give us the gift of spiritual sight. Our vision is all too clouded by the chronic sight of our own and others' needs. Christian hope is often in conflict with that which is visible in the present. Just as faith is "the assurance of things hoped for, the conviction of things not seen" (Heb 11:1 NRSV), so we "hope for what we do not see" (Rom 8:25 NRSV). It's very hard for us to believe that what we do not see is more important, more life-determining, than what we do see. Though utterly determinative of our life, and utterly real, the victory of Christ is veiled to the world's eyes beyond the confines of history and the walls of perplexing problems and pain. Since we are very much in the world, it is often veiled to our eyes as well. Christian spirituality depends on learning how to see properly.

The messianic promise of recovery of sight to the blind must not be totally spiritualized. It is an extraordinary gift when those who have been physically blind are enabled to see. I once visited an Indian village where a mobile eye surgery team had converted a school room into a cataract clinic. Under the light of miners' lamps they removed cataracts from the eyes of dozens of people. A few days later, when the bandages were removed, the joy of those who had been ostracized and rendered helpless by blindness, and now could see, was indescribable.

Paul was blinded on the road to Damascus in order that he might see Christ. One of the most insightful students to whom I've ever taught theology is a woman in Scotland who has been blind from birth. Her descriptions of the nature and character of God reflect profound insight and wisdom. Blinded in her natural sight, she has cultivated a spiritual sight that gives her true perception. The deepest hope of this woman is that one day she will be able to gaze upon God face to face. "Now we see but a poor reflection as in a mirror; then we will see face to face. Now I know in part; then I shall know fully, even as I am fully known" (1 Cor 13:12).

For those of us who are spiritually blind, God gives us sight. Yet cultivating our sight, as with developing all our spiritual senses, requires devotion and discipline. Mention the word *discipline* in reference to the spiritual life, and immediately immense misunderstanding can arise. Spiritual discipline isn't a dutiful, self-willed effort to gain something that we don't have. Rather, it is the joyous delight of learning how to live, and indeed how to use, all that we've been given. As God awakens in us an awareness of all he has accomplished *for* us and *in* us in Christ, we hunger to respond with our whole being. Through discipline, we allow the Spirit of God to plant our lives ever more fully in the gracious "soil" of the life of Christ, so that God might grow in us the fruit of his Spirit.

It is tragic that so many people feel guilty about their spiritual "discipline." Very few people feel satisfied with it. We are constantly besieged by feelings of guilt and failure. All that I've said about the joy of a Christ-centered spirituality can evaporate under the strenuous effort of made spiritual life.

Some seek to rationalize this by deriding the value of spiritual disciplines. David Hume sums up much of the common impression of spiritual discipline in the following derisive comment:

Celibacy, fasting, penance, mortification, self-denial, humility, silence, solitude, and the whole train of monkish virtues:—for what reason are they everywhere rejected by men of sense, but because they serve to no manner of purpose; neither advance a man's fortune in the world, nor render him a more valuable member of society; neither qualify him for the entertainment of company, nor increase his power of self-enjoyment? We observe, on the contrary, that they cross all these desirable ends; stupefy the understanding and harden the heart, obscure the fancy and sour the temper. . . . A gloomy, hare-brained enthusiast . . . will scarcely ever be admitted, when alive, into intimacy and society, except by those who are as delirious and dismal as himself.[5]

Despite Hume's negative assessment, most things that we do require training and discipline. Why should the cultivation of spiritual senses be different? We receive instruction about cooking through cookbooks, magazines and even TV shows, about shopping through consumer magazines and relentless advertisements. We work hard at learning a hobby—whether it is woodworking, car mechanics, knitting, computers, music or horseback riding—by reading books and taking classes. We take lessons, exams, practice and learn from experts. We admire the carefully trained expertise of musicians, artists and athletes.

Praised by a BBC interviewer for his marvelous voice, Luciano Pavarotti gave the following compelling response: "Don't praise me for the instrument. God made it. All I did was to have the discipline to learn how to play it."

Why, when it comes to our relational life—marriage, parenting and spirituality—do we seldom receive training or expect to have to refine our skills through practice? Instead we learn by trial and error. As a result, much of our behavior isn't formed by our beliefs. Dallas Willard asserts, "Once the individual has through divine initiative become alive to God and his Kingdom, the extent of integration of his or her total being into that Kingdom order significantly depends upon the individual's initiative."[6] Though I agree with the essence of Willard's statement, I think it would more adequately reflect the wonder of our life in Christ to say that "the extent of integration of one's total being into that Kingdom order significantly depends upon one's constant response to God's constant initiative."

Willard quotes the following statement by Oswald Chambers on the importance of developing spiritual "habits":

> The question of forming habits on the basis of the grace of God is a very vital one. To ignore it is to fall into the snare of the Pharisee— the grace of God is praised, Jesus Christ is praised, Redemption is praised, but the practical everyday life evades working it out. If we refuse to practice, it is not God's grace that fails when a crisis comes, but our own nature. . . . The practicing is ours, not God's. God regenerates us and puts us in contact with all His divine resources, but He cannot make us walk according to His will.[7]

God can't make us walk according to his will. Nevertheless, as Paul says in Philippians 2:13, "God is at work within you to make you willing and able to fulfill his purposes" (Phillips). God chooses not to *make* us walk according to his will. But he will make us *willing* to so walk, and then give us the *ability* to do his will.

The discipline of learning to see begins with knowing what we are looking for. Spiritual discipline often seems to us to be hard and painful because it has to begin with the equivalent of cleansing the temple. Our lives are as cluttered as a busy marketplace, preoccupied with buying and selling. Our sight is filled with all that we seek to accomplish, produce and acquire. Lest we attempt to subvert God into a cosmic supplier and distributor, who acts in response to our every whim, the Spirit enters our lives with his overturning, cleansing discipline.

After all, everyone is in the process of spiritual formation. We are all becoming something. Formation isn't an option. The only option is what form we are becoming. "Life is, by its very nature, spiritual formation. The question is not *whether* to undertake spiritual formation; the question is *what kind* of spiritual formation are we engaged in. Are we being in ingly conformed to the world, or are we being increasingly conformed to the image of Christ?"[8]

Many people react against this idea of formation, for it suggests that our lives are controlled or determined from outside ourselves. Yet it is only pride in our illusory independence that sustains our illusion of self-control. There is no such thing. We are indeed not completely in our own control. "Genuine spiritual formation brings about a radical shift from being our own production to being God's workmanship."[9]

Living in Christ does indeed require being yoked to him. Yet Jesus says, "Take my yoke upon you and learn from me, for I am gentle and humble in heart, and you will find rest for your souls. For my yoke is easy and my burden is light" (Mt 11:29-30). John reminds us, "His commands are not burdensome" (1 Jn 5:3).

Rather than only stressing the cost of discipline, we do well to remind ourselves of the costs of an undisciplined life. Søren Kierkegaard notes, "It costs a man just as much or even more to go to hell than to come to heaven. Narrow, exceedingly narrow is the way to perdition."[10] In fact, as Dean Inge comments, "a more reasonable estimate of human costs and values will lead us to think that no labour is better expended than that which explores the way to the treasure-house of the spirit, and shows mankind where to find those goods which are increased by being shared, and which none can take from us."[11]

Beatific Vision or Bountiful Blessing?

The vision of God has traditionally been the most treasured goal of Christian spirituality. The highest human aspiration was to gaze on God's face, to kiss God's feet. "Blessed are the pure in heart," Jesus says, "for they will see God" (Mt 5:8).

Life can hold no greater joy than to be in God's presence. Yet few people today would hold that as their highest aspiration. The word *vision* has become so commonplace as to have almost lost its meaning. Everyone and everything has "vision"—and the purpose of "vision" is blessing.

The bountiful blessing has usurped the beatific vision as the goal of life. Banks and beauty parlors, jails and jewelry stores all have their "vision" and "mission statements" posted at their entrance. Politicians have formed charitable foundations dedicated to funding visions of a better future.

The very foundation of our faith is at issue in our discussion of spiritual sight. What is the dominant determinant of our life, faith and spirituality? We all tend to be like Thomas: "Show me Jesus' hands and side and then I will believe" (see Jn 20:25). Our faith is founded on what we can see, and thus our spirituality is a spirituality for results, and our ministry is a ministry for results.

While serving on the pastoral staff of a large church, I was told that one of my responsibilities was to produce large, highly visible, successful programs that would regularly attract a large number of people. In such a church, continuing in ministry depends on producing visible successes.

If faith is the assurance of things hoped for and confidence in things unseen, then antifaith is finding assurance only in what we already have and placing our confidence only in what we can see. If true understanding is to know that the world was formed by the Word of God and what is seen was made from that which is unseen, then misunderstanding—or actually *antiunderstanding*—is the notion that the world is formed by our efforts.

Spiritual faith is the confidence that the heart of reality is the relational communion of the blessed Holy Trinity. What we're given in Christ is our adopted participation in that communion. "This is eternal life," Jesus prays: "that they may know you, the only true God, and Jesus Christ, whom you have sent . . . as you are in me and I am in you. May they also be in us so that the world may believe that you have sent me" (Jn 17:3, 21).

On the other hand, material faith (or antifaith) claims that the heart of reality is evidenced only in visible results. What you see is what you get. Productivity, accomplishment and experience compose the unblessed "material trinity" at whose shrines we daily bow.

Obviously God wants us to "taste and see that he is good." Obviously God has prepared for us good works in which we are to walk. But God would have our motivation and our desired goal not to be the tasting and seeing, and not the accomplishing and the walking, but *God himself.*

A dear, critically ill friend recently told me of a conversation he had had with God. In the middle of the night he awoke, flooded with dismay over his illness. He prayed, "Lord, all my life I've sought to serve you, but now I can't do anything. I don't even have energy to walk. I can barely talk. I'm so frustrated."

He recounted to me that he heard the Lord ask, "What have you preached all these years?"

"Everywhere I've gone I've proclaimed and written that our chief end is to glorify you and enjoy you forever."

"Bruce," the Lord replied, "you can do that even from bed. You don't have to write any books, preach any sermons or organize any ministries to do that."

Our "chief end" is singular. It is God himself. What greater end could anyone have?

I mentioned in the previous chapter the baptism I observed of a blind former Hindu in India. He was ostracized by his community for becoming a Christian and abandoning his decades-long religious devotion to Krishna. If he could have seen what he was leaving—status, class, social respect—his choice might have seemed absurd. What nonsense to exchange that, through immersion in a pool of scummy water, for life as an outcast! Yet his face said it all as he emerged from the water. Joy, joy, uncontainable joy! Faith is confidence in things unseen.

Pay Attention

The challenge before us is clear. How do we live with complete confidence in the "unseen" in the midst of the visible, attention-captivating world? The answer is also clear. Spiritual sight reverses the normal flow of vision. We are freed to let what we don't see give meaning to what we do see, and to let what we do see point us to what we don't see. Our material sight can be transformed by grace into a healthy stimulus for our spiritual sight.

Father Anthony of Egypt, a fourth-century desert monk, had the following advice in response to the question "What must I do to please God?"

Pay attention to what I tell you: whoever you may be, always have God before your eyes; whatever you do, do it according to the testimony of the holy Scriptures; in whatever place you live, do not easily leave it. Keep these three precepts and you will be saved.[12]

Anthony's advice is as appropriate for our twentieth-century urban jungles as for the fourth-century Egyptian desert. First, cultivating "spiritual sight" requires developing attentiveness. "Pay attention," Anthony says. We are so quickly and easily distracted. We must choose to be attentive to God. It requires effort. "Always have God before your eyes." We can let what we see be a vehicle to carry us to the heart of the One whom we can't see.

Second, "whatever you do, do it according to the testimony of the holy Scriptures." We can let the Bible form and inform our perception of life, rather than letting our perceptions form our understanding of the Bible. Unless the Bible tunes our senses, it is likely that the "words" that we "see, hear, taste, smell and feel" will be the fruit of our own or other people's fancy, rather than the Word of God.

Finally, "in whatever you place you live, do not easily leave it." Wandering eyes, hearts and lives are some of our biggest obstacles to the development of spiritual vision. When we move too quickly, we can't help being consumed by the demands of our surroundings. Once our surroundings become familiar and even routine, we can focus more fully on what is unseen.

Over a period of seven years, my family underwent four international moves. During those years much of our attention had to be focused on our surroundings, on issues of language and culture and shopping. Our prayers were for patience, perseverance and survival. What we saw determined the concerns of our spiritual life, rather than what we didn't see, the Lord God, determining the concerns for our material life.

Though we experienced great growth in those initial months in new locations, once we were able to settle down we grew even more. We found it took about two years in one place for this to occur. Thus over seven years we needed eight years to become settled! No wonder Anthony says, "Don't easily leave the place where you live."

Walk Slowly

Grace, a woman in our church who for forty years had an awe-inspiring ministry to street people in Seattle, told me her simple key to effective ministry: "If you want to have ministry on the streets, then walk slowly and it will happen to you. If you want to avoid it, then walk fast."

Grace's advice is also relevant to the development of spiritual sight. If we want to learn to see the presence of God, we need to walk slowly. Spiritual directors call this the spiritual act of "noticing."

When people bump into us, we say, "Watch where you're going!" Most of us don't notice our spiritual surroundings. We're so busy watching what we're leaving (our failures, guilt and triumphs) or what we're trying to get to (our hopes, fears and dreams) that we don't notice where we are now. As a result, we miss seeing the signs of the presence of God all around us.

There are some simple keys to developing the art of spiritual noticing. They all depend on curiosity, and that is probably why Jesus said, "To enter the kingdom you must be like little children" (see Lk 18:17). More than the presumed innocence of children, entering the kingdom requires curiosity. Curiosity involves noticing what's around us, asking questions of it and delighting in discovery.

Taking our dogs for a walk through the forest near our home is always an amusing adventure. Undaunted by rain, the younger dog charges up and down the hillsides, passionately exploring pathways that are not apparent to human eyes. Her curiosity is abundant, but her speed often drives her past subtle sights and smells. Our other dog, an elderly, long-time family companion, is content to plod along with her nose to the ground. Her curiosity extends no farther than a few inches before her face. Apparently what she finds there is very captivating, for her nose constantly gets stuck in fascinating smells. She needs no eyes and is oblivious to the sights of the verdant forest.

If we want to notice the surrounding signs of the presence of God, we need to walk more slowly and notice what we see. Spiritual sight is the carefully cultivated capacity of the theological detective. How can we see the activity of the Unseen in the midst of the seen? When he was asked why most people were not good detectives, Sherlock Holmes replied, "You see, but you do not observe." The hurry that crowds the lives of urban residents often blinds us from seeing God's presence. An essential discipline for cultivating spiritual sight is to take time to walk more slowly. There is no other option.

Upon noticing, we need to cultivate the capacity to *observe* what we see by asking questions such as

☐ What do I see in this of the hand of God?

☐ What are God's purposes in this?

☐ What is God doing, and how do I participate in the fulfillment of his purposes?

One question that I never tire of asking people is "What do you see God doing in your current situation?" Another way of phrasing the same question is to ask, "If God was asking you to write a 'Book of the Acts of God' for our region and time, as Luke did for the first century, what would you want to include?" It is unceasingly fascinating to see what others are noticing!

We would do well to pray daily certain prayers of saints who cultivated spiritual sight. The daily prayer of fourth-century St. Patrick, for example, forms a good guide:

Today I arise, invoking the Blessed Trinity,
Confessing the Blessed Unity, Creator of all things that be.
Lord Jesus the Christ, today surround me with thy might;
Before, behind, on left and right, be thou in breadth, in length,
    in height.
Direct and control the minds of all who think on me,
The lips of all who speak to me, the eyes of all who look on me.
Christ be with me, Christ within me, Christ behind me,
    Christ before me;
Christ beside me, Christ to win me, Christ to comfort and restore me;
Christ beneath me, Christ above me, Christ in quiet, Christ
    in danger;
Christ in hearts of all that love me, Christ in mouth of friend
    and stranger.

Another good possibility is a prayer found in the sixteenth-century Celtic *Book of Hours:*

> God be in my head, and in my understanding;
> God be in mine eyes, and in my looking;
> God be in my mouth, and in my speaking;
> God be in my heart, and in my thinking;
> God be at mine end, and at my departing.

Hearing Truth

The Gospels frequently record Jesus saying, "Let those who have ears listen." The only people I've met without ears were leprosy patients. I have a few friends who are deaf and read lips and sign. I've also met many people who have their hearing *and* their ears but are still deaf.

Sometimes God has to shout at us to get our attention. The whispers of his love and the songs of his blessings are unheard by many spiritually deaf lives. It often takes the shout of suffering to remind us to take heed to his voice, and usually then our response is bitterness and indignation over God's apparent lack of compassion or power.

Even for Christians, spiritual hearing is often dulled. We usually refer to Revelation 3:20 in evangelistic sermons: "Listen! I am standing at the door, knocking; if you hear my voice and open the door, I will come in to you and eat with you, and you with me" (NRSV). Yet the context of this verse shows that it was written to Christians, to the church in Laodicea. This was a church whose faith was not put to work, whose lives were lukewarm, whose sense of need was dulled by riches. It couldn't see its nakedness and shame. God was calling to it to return and be clothed, to receive anointing to see again, to repent. So God says, "Listen!"

For this reason Scripture calls us to enter into training. "Train yourself to be godly. For physical training is of some value, but godliness has value for all things, holding promise for both the present life and the life to come" (1 Tim 4:7-8; also see Heb 5:14; 12:11; 2 Pet 2:14). Musicians train their ears to hear the right notes. People acquiring other languages must train their ears as well as their tongues. Learning to hear God's voice, too, requires training. Sometimes we listen best through adversity, when other noises have been silenced.

"Who's There?"

Our capacity to hear is diminished as our senses are dulled by the values, perspectives and expectations of our surrounding society. The decibels of desire are turned up so loudly in our world that they easily drown out the call of God to join him at the kingdom feast. In the United States, for example, it's estimated that in 1900 there were fewer than three hundred different kinds of products for people to buy. Today there are millions, and just one of our hyperstores is stocked with over seventy thousand different products. The average American now spends 9 percent of his or her nonworking, nonsleeping hours gathering information about products and at least six hours a week shopping. Clearly Descartes was wrong and the California bumper sticker is right: "I shop, therefore I am."

God knocks at those points where he is shut out of our lives and we are imprisoned within, imprisoned by some bondage which does not allow us to be free in God's love and in God's will for our wholeness in our life with others.[13]

Often the only sounds that catch our attention are cries of pain. As George MacDonald eloquently said, "There are two doorkeepers to the house of prayer, and Sorrow is more on the alert to open than her grandson Joy."[14] If we rest confidently in the goodness of God, when Sorrow knocks our first impulse can be to open the door. In so doing we can hear God's voice and receive God's embrace. "There lies a prayer in every spirit, generally frozen, sometimes only dumb, *to be taken like a child,* and weakness lets it out sometimes."[15]

There is a simple discipline required if we are to grow in our spiritual hearing. When we meet pain or pleasure, discouragement or delight, envy or anxiety, our first question needs to be "Who's there?" We need to receive whatever is knocking at our lives as an invitation to join Christ at his feast. Before we ask the why question—"Why did this happen to me?"—or the what question—"What am I going to do?"—we need to ask "Who's there?" and join Christ at the table.

I've already mentioned some of the lessons I've learned in an intensive-care "classroom." Between the ferryboat dream I've described and the reminder I received about my "chief end" through the Westminster Shorter Catechism, I had another significant experience.

After I had rejected the nurse's offer of a sleeping pill and she'd left the room, I lay on my bed. I certainly wasn't going anywhere, with twelve tubes connected to my partially paralyzed body. I thought about my dream. Realizing that I had nearly died, and realizing also that my life priorities had been wrong, I wanted another chance to live differently. At that point I heard a knock on the door.

I mumbled, "Come in," but no one entered.

That's strange, I thought. *Who knocks on an intensive-care room door at one in the morning?*

I heard another knock, and I responded more forcefully, "Come in."

Just then my spiritual ears were opened for a moment, and I heard, "Tim, let me in." The meaning was clear. Christ wanted to join me at the "table" of my hospital bed, transforming it into a place of communion.

Recognizing the Right Voice

Legitimate anxieties are raised when someone speaks of "hearing voices." Questions of sanity are posed, as are questions about the demonic. We know there are spiritual voices besides God's clamoring for our attention. We know we are capable of talking ourselves into believing just about anything. How do we know it's *his* voice when we hear it?

We can assume familiarity and be profoundly mistaken. Like most parents, my wife and I know our children very well. But on the phone, much to the amusement of our three daughters, we can't immediately tell their voices apart. How do we know, then, with whom we are speaking?

Recognizing the right voice requires knowing the character and the characteristics of the one to whom we are listening. After my wife or I have listened for a few seconds, we can identify which daughter is speaking on the phone. That's because we know the interests, concerns and activities of each of them. In the same way, as God's people, we need to let the character of God clarify for us the identity of the voice we hear.

Every pastor in the Western world is flooded with advertisements for programs and resources that will make his or her ministry more successful. Upon retirement to a small church in England, after a lifetime of service in India, Bishop Lesslie Newbigin made an insightful comment on the promotional mail he began receiving: "What a pity that Jesus did not have some professionally qualified experts in public relations to help him! He could have avoided crucifixion."[16]

Fortunately, there is a profound objectivity to spiritual hearing. We don't just hear our own words or random spiritual voices. We don't simply erect giant receiving dishes, like NASA, and gather whatever noise comes from spiritual outer (or even inner) space. God is the Word, and he has spoken clearly and definitively in writing and in life. We need to learn how to hear God's Word in Scripture. This gives an objectivity to our spirituality. There is more to Christian spirituality than our experience, our feelings, our "voices." We are participants in a great drama and need to hear, know and even memorize the lines. Paul exhorts Timothy, "Give attention to the . . . reading of scripture" (1 Tim 4:13 NRSV). That is, be present when you read. So often we read without thinking, merely to check "Bible reading" off our list of required duties.

A fascinating form of hearing Scripture is practiced by a friend of ours who is a professor of theology in Cambridge, as well as an exceptionally talented musician. He gathers a group of musicians, with their instruments, for a Bible study. He will ask them to "envision" the passage with their ears. What does it sound like? What is its music? For example, they might be studying Jesus' baptism by John, as recorded in Matthew 3. The violinist might play the sound of the wilderness, the trumpetist the music of John crying in the wilderness, the flutist the entrance of Jesus, the oboist the dialogue between Jesus and John, and the clarinetist the descent of the dove. Studying the passage with their ears and instruments brings it to life for them in a fresh way.

Spiritual listening requires reading the Bible not as an object to be analyzed but as a subject that analyzes *us* as its object. We are to read for transformation, rather than mere information. Robert Mulholland provides the following helpful distinction between informational and formational reading. He suggests that in our reading of Scripture, both approaches are essential if we are indeed to hear God's Word.[17]

Informational Reading	Formational Reading
Goal: Read as much as possible	**Goal:** Read as meaningfully as possible
Process: Linear—speed as priority	**Process:** Horizontal—depth as priority
Subject: Reader is in control and seeks to master the Bible as the "object" of study	**Subject:** God is in control and seeks to master the reader as the "object" of study
Style: Analysis, criticism	**Style:** Reverence, humility
Orientation: Solve problems and seek solutions	**Orientation:** Deepen relationship and seek God

As we grow to understand the character of the God to whom we long to listen, we will cultivate the capacity to recognize his voice amid the din that assaults our senses. So doing requires reverent, humble determination. C. S. Lewis describes this well:

> The real problem of the Christian comes where people do not usually look for it. It comes the very moment you wake up each morning. All your wishes and hopes for the day rush at you like wild animals. And the first job each morning consists simply in shoving them all back; in listening to that other voice, taking that other point of view, letting that other larger, stronger, quieter life come flowing in.[18]

As we grow in our ability to "shove back" all the other voices, more and more space is created in our lives to hear God's voice. As this occurs, our creative boldness in denouncing alternative voices increases. Os Guinness relates an overheard conversation between a KGB agent and an elderly woman in a Russian Orthodox church. Seeing the woman passionately kissing the feet of a statue of Jesus, he asked, "Are you also prepared to kiss the feet of our beloved Party Secretary?"

She replied, "Why of course, but only if you crucify him first."[19]

Obeying What We Hear

Our spiritual hearing will improve only as we obey the truth we hear. Disobedience to the truth deafens. More than deafening us, disobedience renders us dumb. The word *absurd* comes from the Latin *surd,* which means deaf. *Obedient* comes from the Latin *audire,* which means listening. In Scripture, to hear is indeed to obey. Even in reference to God we are given the assurance that if we pray according to God's will, our prayers will be granted. "This is the confidence we have in approaching God: that if we ask anything according to his will, he hears us. And if we know that he hears us—whatever we ask—we know that we have what we asked of him" (1 Jn 5:14-15).

The absurdly disobedient lives rampant in our society result from spiritual deafness. Henri Nouwen comments, "A spiritual discipline is necessary in order to move slowly from an absurd to an obedient life, from a life filled with noisy worries to a life in which there is some free inner space where we can listen to our God and follow his guidance."[20]

A few years ago my family attended a marvelous memorial service for a very godly great-aunt. The testimonies of her kindness and character were extravagant but appropriate. Following the service, I overheard one of my relatives say to another, "In comparison, your memorial service will be very short, won't it!"

As scathing as the comment was, it conveyed truth. There probably wouldn't have been many nice things said in this other person's memory. But the remarkable fact of this story is not the audacious comment but its consequences. This relative heard the truth, and her life changed. The entire family began to notice striking evidences of kindness and humility. A few years later this person's memorial service was indeed a joyous celebration of her character and conduct.

Our capacity to hear is cultivated by the community of God's people. Just as hearing is made objective through the Word, so it is objectified through the voices of others. Though at times God may speak to us through words of chastisement coming from others, as in the case of my family member, more typically we help others hear most fully through our praise. We desperately need the supportive encouragement of others, words of affirmation whispered relentlessly in our ears, if we are to redirect our hearing away from the noises that distract us from God.

Just as others' affirmation helps retune our hearing, even more effective is our praise of God. It is said that the chaffinch loses its beautiful song if it is captured and taken indoors. If fact, if its songlessness continues, it will become depressed and die. So with us: regardless of whether our song is beautiful, making a joyful noise is basic to our spiritual health.

My wife and I experienced singing as spiritual food while visiting a group of missionaries along the Thai-Cambodian border. Their daily activities put them at continual risk, as they served Cambodian refugees in the war zones along the border. Their spiritual nourishment was to gather several times a week to sing and pray. One day we were privileged to join them. As mortar shells exploded in the distance, we sang and sang and sang. I've seldom heard people sing with such passion. The choice was to sing or get depressed and die. Their singing opened their (and our) ears to hear more fully the voice of God, and set them free to live in radical obedience.

Obedience sometimes is radical and costly, as in the case of these battle-zone relief workers. Usually, for most of us, it is mundane and ordinary. Both kinds of obedience require hearing the right Word if we are to live the right life. Our capacity to hear and obey in the grand moments is formed in our obedience in the mundane.

Hearing God's voice in the midst of the ordinary things of life can provide us with daily companionship and pleasure. In this way we can learn the wondrous freedom of having such confidence in God that we need not take ourselves, or our circumstances, with dread-filled seriousness. We can relax. All does not depend on us. Once we hear God's gracious, sovereign, present Voice, once we grow in our discovery of his companionship in our daily pleasures and pains, we can abandon our futile attempts to be in control of our lives and circumstances. And we can abandon our equally futile attempts to hide our inadequacies. We can laugh again.

We come to recognize that there is music in the spheres. We can hear the birds sing, even in the midst of violence and dismay. That softer, quieter, more solid and more Real Voice is heard all around us as a reminder that we're not alone, we're not orphaned, more goodness is yet to come.

In his inimitable way, Garrison Keillor describes this by saying that "woofing is not the last word":

> To know and to serve God, of course, is why we're here, a clear truth that, like the nose on your face, is near at hand and easily discernible but can make you dizzy if you try to focus on it hard. But a little faith will see you through. . . . When the country goes temporarily to the dogs, cats must learn to be circumspect, walk on fences, sleep in trees, and have faith that all this woofing is not the last word. What is the last word then? Gentleness is everywhere in daily life, a sign that faith rules through ordinary things: through cooking and small talk, through storytelling, making love, fishing, tending animals and sweet corn and flowers, through sports, music and books, raising kids—all the places where the grave soaks in and grace shines through.[21]

As our eyes and ears are opened, we are set free to see and hear grace shining through all that surrounds us!

4
Smelling, Tasting & Touching Truth

SOME MIGHT SUGGEST THAT BY CONSIDERING OUR SENSE OF SMELL IN A BOOK about spirituality I'm getting carried away with my metaphor. Sight and sound make sense, but *smell?* However, I'm following a strong biblical precedent:

> But thanks be to God, who always leads us in triumphal procession in Christ and through us spreads everywhere the fragrance of the knowledge of him. For we are to God the aroma of Christ among those who are being saved and those who are perishing. To the one we are the smell of death; to the other, the fragrance of life. And who is equal to such a task? (2 Cor 2:14-16)

Apparently the sense of smell plays a vital role in our spiritual formation. Except in Protestantism, incense is used in most of the world's ways of worship. Not only does it symbolize prayer and our longing to rise up toward God, but it also provides a perfume: the sweet aroma of the divine penetrating our lives.

The Mysterious Aroma

Smell is basic to life, and thus it carries behind it a spiritual sense. Nobody's smell is neutral. We are either pleasant or putrid, provocative or pungent. According to Paul, we smell either like life or like death. And our smell is not a perfume we purchase and put on.

I remember vividly the Sunday I sat in church next to a person whose perfume was so strong that it was all I could do to force myself to worship. Fortunately, spiritual scents can't be overliberally applied from bottles. They come from within us, the fruit of our being. People smell either like the coming Christ or like the approaching chaos.

Paul's surprise for us in the 2 Corinthians passage I've quoted is that the same aroma doesn't smell the same way to different people. What smells pleasant and life-giving to one person may smell repulsive and deadly to another. Thus cultivating our spiritual sense of smell, and the resulting spiritual scent, is foundational to Christian spirituality.

I've never read a book on this topic. Most people apparently have better sense than I do. Yet I want to smell like Christ. I want to be part of a church that smells like Christ. I want our world to smell like him.

While serving as a pastor, one day I received a call from a colleague at church asking me to come quickly to meet with a very distressed man. As Henry told me his story, I learned that he had determined to commit suicide the previous Saturday night but had decided to give himself an "extension" in order to attend our church on Sunday. He'd never been to church before, didn't understand anything that went on, but was captivated.

He said, "I sensed there was something different there, and I couldn't tell what. I gave myself another twenty-four-hour extension to see if anyone could explain it. So here I am."

I knew that Henry's capacity to understand was muddled by his distress and that my response had better be clear and quick if this man's life was to be saved, both physically and spiritually. He had mentioned that he was a scientist at the local university. For over ten years he'd been chronically depressed, had sought for God but not found him, and had decided that life wasn't worth living. Thus suicide!

I said to him, "Henry, you're a scientist. What percentage of all that there is to know in the universe would you say you know?"

He replied, "Only a very tiny fraction."

"And in that tiny percentage, you've found no evidence for God?"

"Right," he said.

"And based on that small amount you know, you are willing to make the judgment that God doesn't exist in the other 99.9999999 percent?"

"Yes."

"That's fairly poor scientific reasoning, isn't it?" I boldly suggested.

"Well actually, putting it that way, you're right," he said.

"Henry, why not try an experiment? Let me outline a thirty-day research project to help you explore a tiny portion of the other 99.9999999 percent. If after this research you don't find any evidence for God, then all you've endured is another thirty days of depression. You then can decide what to do about your life. If you do find evidence, then you can decide what to do with God. How does that sound?"

"OK, I'm willing," he replied, with curiosity.

I then outlined the components of a thirty-day experiment: daily prayer and Bible study, the reading of some key books, a small group fellowship with other Christian men, and a ministry to street kids through which Henry could give his life away. He agreed. He prayed with me that if there was a God, he would make himself known. I then called a friend who led the small group, asking him if he could meet Henry for lunch.

What Henry had sensed (smelled?) that Sunday was the presence of Jesus Christ. And after thirty days of "hanging out" with Christ and with Christians, Henry did indeed find Life, a reason for living, and he began to smell like Christ. The experiment was a success. He had entered my office smelling of death. He found the sweet aroma of life in Jesus Christ.

The Contagious Aroma

Praise God for the privilege of belonging to a church that smells like Christ and saves people's lives by the very scent. C. S. Lewis relates in *The Screwtape Letters* how a senior devil admonishes his apprentice junior devil to keep his "patient" out of the home of a particular Christian family. "The whole place reeks of that deadly odour. . . . Even guests, after a weekend visit, carry some of the smell away with them. The dog and the cat are tainted with it."[1]

We can't make ourselves smell like Christ. It's an aroma that we must pick up by being with him.

Anyone who has ever visited a Third World slum has discovered olfactory capacities previously unknown. My wife and I drove through an indescribably horrific *bustee* in Calcutta, where all our senses were assaulted by poverty and decay. Rounding a corner, we passed through a gateway and drove into one of the compounds of the Missionaries of Charity. There we were overwhelmed by contrasting sights, sounds and scents. The scent of brightly blooming flowers filled the air. The sounds of the sisters singing in chapel greeted our ears. The sight of orphans, widows and leprosy patients receiving loving care filled our eyes with tears. Surely we had just passed out of the gates of hell onto the threshold of paradise.

We can't fabricate such scents on our own. They come through unconditional surrender of our bodies to Christ, as we present our bodies—our senses—as living sacrifices (Rom 12:1). They also come as we do this together, corporately, as the body of Christ.

The Missionaries of Charity had made such a corporate surrender. I asked the mother superior, "Are the sisters ever afraid for their lives as they venture out into the *bustee* to provide care?"

"Of course," was her prompt reply.

"How do they deal with their fear?" I asked.

"Oh," she said rather matter-of-factly, "they're prepared to die!"

Taste and See That the Lord Is Good

It's not simply that the quickest way to a person's heart is through the stomach. Nor is it simply an agreement with Ludwig Feuerbach's materialistic assertion that "we are what we eat." But I'm convinced that God wants to feast us on truth we can *taste*. In a culture deafened by noise, satiated on plenty yet starving for truth, we need our spiritual appeti~~c~~ whetted. Of the making of many words there is no end. Our wordy w needs truth that can be tasted.

There's no place more appropriate to talk about the sense of taste than a society in which a near majority have eating disorders. It seems we all eat too much of the wrong things, or too much of the right things, or not enough of anything. Yet apparently this isn't a new phenomenon. An ancient Egyptian papyrus is reputed to read, "Man eats too much. Thus he lives on only a quarter of what he consumes. The doctors, however, live on the remaining three-quarters."[2]

Those who are concerned with others' spiritual growth need to spend more time whetting others' appetites. We need to prepare—in our lives, in our Christian gatherings and in our daily interactions with others—delicious, beautifully presented feasts.

To celebrate our daughter's high-school graduation, some friends gave us the gift of dinner at a French restaurant. We dined for three hours with our three daughters. Not only was the food extraordinarily delicious, but it was also an art form of beauty and careful design.

One of the reasons for our spiritual anorexia is that the food presented before us is not appetizing, nutritious or attractive. So many Christian worship services are poorly prepared and hastily thrown together. Pastors will spend twenty hours preparing their twenty-minute sermon but devote only twenty minutes to preparation of the other forty minutes of worship. Flowers, choirs, robes and rooms may be carefully prepared, but the heart of the feast to which we're inviting people is often "pulled off the shelf" and rapidly prepared with little creativity or effort. Spiritual fast food will never suffice.

While living in Scotland, we were invited to dine at our local laird's home. He and his family were lords of the manor, owning the eighteen thousand acres that surrounded our stone cottage. We anticipated that meal for days, skimped on lunch to guard our appetite and arrived promptly in eager anticipation of a delightful evening and delicious meal. Needless to say, we were not disappointed!

We've already discussed God's gift to us of the sacraments as visible and material words. Through these "material words" that we can see, taste and touch, we hear the voice of God. He is the Bread of Life come to our world.

We eat his flesh and drink his blood. The common, ordinary foc
of life, a bite of bread and a sip of juice, become for us the incarnate body
of the Son of God.

Western Christians are often criticized for being materialistic. Legitimate denunciations of our prosperity gospels and our preoccupation with
our own comfort abound. But actually the tragedy of much of our evangelical Christian piety is not that we are too materialistic but that in a
particular way we are not materialistic enough. We have consigned God
to a "spiritual" realm and focus the gospel on "saving" and encouraging
"souls." As a result, many Christians approach their bodies, their possessions and the earth itself as if these had no relation to a divine Lord and
a "spiritual" presence. Many Christians have left the material realm without a Ruler and thus feel free to do with it as they please. The only
presence of God many expect to find among their possessions is in the
form of *presents*. We want to find God's provision but aren't so sure we
want to find his sovereign, reigning presence.

God, however, has shown us his face in a human body. Creaturely forms
can convey to us the grace of God. In Christ the spiritual God has made
himself perfectly available in material flesh. Not only did he demonstrate
his perfect availability in the incarnate life of Christ, but he also mani-
fested his perfect authority over all things material and spiritual. No
wonder Jesus scandalized the religious world by his merrymaking, eating
and drinking with outcasts. No wonder his followers have been con-
demned as cannibals and flesh-eaters as they enacted his command to "eat
my flesh and drink my blood." Something about it strikes us as definitely
"unspiritual."

Jesus commanded us to remind ourselves every time we eat bread and
drink wine that he has worn our flesh. He gave us as reminders things
that we touch everyday—common food—to call us continually to himself.
Bread, water and wine express to us the triune God's perfect response to
himself in Christ's obedient baptism and in his loving self-offering on the
cross. Every time we eat, we are to be delivered from all common forms
of religiosity that focus on what we must do in order to make ourselves
acceptable to God. Each meal can remind us that our lives have been

made acceptable because of what the Incarnate God has done on our behalf, in our flesh.

When we begin to have our appetite stimulated and desire to encounter God in material ways, the most mundane moments can become meeting places with God. Even something as mundane as eating can be spiritual! No wonder the two refugee disciples who were fleeing Jerusalem for Emmaus following Jesus' crucifixion recognized the "stranger" who accompanied them on the road only when they ate together. It was in the breaking of the bread that they recognized him (Lk 24:35). For us too, meals can be divine meetings, places where we become aware once again (re-cognize) that God is with us.

Banquet Spirituality

As we've seen, when Jesus wanted to describe life in the kingdom of God, he often chose the imagery of a party. The kingdom is a feast, a banquet, a celebration. John, in his Revelation, describes the culmination of history as the marriage feast of the Lamb of God with his bride, the church.

People love parties. Much of our time is occupied with what we call recreation and leisure activities: music, entertainment, sports, holidays, food, drink (drugs), hobbies, possessions. But unfortunately, as much as we would like these things to be our life, they are for most of us diversions from life, and eventually we must get back to the "real world." Often we return to work from our recreation exhausted. We awake after our parties with headaches.

The contrast between our moments of play and our daily responsibilities becomes oppressive. When we think of celebration we think of times when we can forget it all, get away for a while, escape and relax. The hardships, complexities and pains of life are left at the door, and we immerse ourselves in fun. But that pursuit inevitably turns back on us. The very vehicles we use to pursue happiness become chains that enslave us, preventing us from celebrating. People become slaves to oppressive jobs in order to pay for their homes and holidays, stereos and ski equipment. Sore muscles and injured bodies indicate that our supposed recreation is often more a form of *decreation*.

What does all this have to do with the disciplines of the spiritual life? Everything! I will repeat what I mentioned earlier. Spiritual disciplines are *tools God has provided which we can use to plant our lives ever more fully in the soil of his grace, that he might grow in us the fruit of his Spirit.* In this way the mundane moments of life as well as the times of terror can be lived as feasts and even celebrations.

Delighting in the banquet requires only a few prerequisites. First, we must be hungry. Thus Jesus says, "Blessed are those who hunger and thirst for righteousness, for they will be filled" (Mt 5:6). The real question in spiritual discipline is not "Are we disciplined enough?" but "Are we hungry enough?"

As we saw in our discussion about the Lord's Supper, the Host, the Provider of the banquet, the Servant at the banquet, and the banquet itself are one—Jesus Christ. Our role is simple: to come hungry, feast, be thankful and go home by a different route. The first three are obvious. The fourth catches us off guard. You can't feast at this banquet and go home the same way you came. Everything is different after you have eaten. You will live forever after as one who has feasted at the King's table. There is an accountability, a status, a representative role that shapes us. If we're thankful for this feast, we'll live differently because of having eaten there.

The kingdom of God is not a two-class society, with a high spiritual class for giants, clergy, missionaries and saints and a lower class for "ordinary Christians." We are all ordinary saints: ordinary because we are all servants of God, saints because in Christ we've become adopted sons and daughters of our heavenly Father. As Peter writes to the whole church: "You are a chosen people, a royal priesthood, a holy nation, a people belonging to God, that you may declare the praises of him who called you out of darkness into his wonderful light" (1 Pet 2:9).

Finding God Through a Donut

This was brought home to me one spring when I was preparing a group of college students for upcoming summer mission trips. As orientation, we went out on the streets of our city to discover side"—to go to those places that we normally avoid. We wanted to see our city's broken points and look there for signs of God's presence. I encouraged the students simply to watch and observe, and not to approach this as an evangelistic mission.

Several students went to a donut shop that at that time was a center of teenage prostitution. Hundreds of street kids sold their bodies in order to survive on the streets. Over donuts and coffee, one college student fell into conversation with a streetwise teen. Two more alien worlds couldn't have met! One a privileged child of the suburbs, experiencing the protection and stimulus of university life, the other a petrified child of the night, experiencing the exploitation and slime of city street life. Yet over their donuts communion occurred. Their lives connected. Soon the student was learning from the street kid, and his heart broke.

He couldn't help but begin to talk about the One who loves with a nonexploitive love, about an embrace that builds up rather than tears down. The donut holes became fitting analogies for empty lives. Soon, over the crumbs on the table, the two were knit in prayer, and the child of the streets received his inheritance as an adopted child of God.

But now what was the student from my church going to do? Was he to leave a Bible tract and say goodby to his new brother in Christ, wishing him a wonderful life? He couldn't bring him back to his dormitory, but he also realized he couldn't just pay the bill and walk alone out the door.

Going to a pay phone, he called his parents, who lived in a nearby affluent suburb, and asked if he could come home for a few days and bring a friend with him. His parents gave their hearty assent, reminding him to bring his dirty laundry and assuring him that any friend of his was a friend of theirs too.

The two moved home and spent a wonderful few weeks as the former street kid delighted in the warmth of a Christian home. Daily Bible studies built his faith, and family meals became a center of healing.

After just two weeks, however, the new family member became critically ill, and the family rushed him to the hospital. Within only a few hours he was on the verge of death from a massive cerebral hemorrhage. Just before he entered the embrace of his heavenly Father, he admonished his weeping brother and adopted parents not to cry for him. "During these last two weeks I've been fed love and life like I've never known before. It's made all the rest of my life worth it, and I can't wait for what's yet to come. I know it's only going to get better. Don't weep for me."

Turning Meals into Celebrations

We "say grace" in our home, neither as a magical ritual nor as a religious duty. An ungraced meal is for us a poorly prepared feast. Giving thanks is foundational to tasting. The food is unprepared without it.

In saying grace we do at least five things. First, we acknowledge the food as a gift and God as the giver. Thus gratitude fills our home. Second, we acknowledge the real gift and its purpose. Christ is the Bread of Life given for the salvation of the world. Third, we recognize that God is present at our table. He is both the host, the provider of the feast, and the feast itself, the One who is our life. Fourth, we affirm that life is to be celebrated in all its fullness. We needn't wait for special feast days to celebrate. The most simple, mundane meal can be transformed into a brief party. God would have us not take ourselves too seriously. We needn't feel as if our lives are so important and our responsibilities so vital that we can't sit down to eat together. We don't have to eat on the run, or in the drive-through, or standing in front of the microwave. We can rest, relax and be nourished. Finally, we affirm our solidarity with the body of Christ. We eat in anticipation of the day when we will feast with that countless host from throughout all time and all the world at the marriage feast of the Lamb of God.

In the final chapter of this book we will look at Christians' role as "appetizers" for the world. We are to live in such a way that when the world bites into us, gets a taste of us, its appetite will be stimulated for more. We are to be hors d'oeuvres of the future kingdom banquet.

Neither the church nor the world needs simply to be admonished to be more disciplined and devoted. Our malnourishment stems rather from lack of hungry desire. Our stomachs have been filled with junk food. It doesn't occur to most of us that the gospel of Christ and the community of his people is where our deepest hungers can be satisfied. God would raise up tasty Christians who themselves have tasted and seen the goodness of God. Having been nourished themselves, they can be feasts for others.

Feeling Truth

I mentioned in the first chapter that God had given me the gift of a very personal icon. Every day when I touch the scar on my stomach, I'm reminded physically of the truth of Galatians 2:20: "I have been crucified with Christ and I no longer live, but Christ lives in me. The life I live in the body, I live by faith in the Son of God, who loved me and gave himself for me."

Weeks after my discharge from the hospital in Alaska, I was taking my first walk down the main street of the town. Life seemed so full and good. The air smelled purer; the sea gulls and even the ravens sounded more melodious. The colors in the stores and on the mountains were more vivid. The warmth of my wife's touch on my arm and our daughter in our arms was so full and penetrating.

The pharmacist emerged from his store. I'd never met him before, but he called me by name. He asked me how I was feeling and then said, "Praise God that you've recovered. You better take good care of yourself. I've a pint of my blood invested in you."

My very life had become for him an icon. His blood given for me—a physical reminder of Christ's blood given for us.

The Passionate God

Throughout this book I've been asserting that God would give us truth we can touch. Our bodies need not be barriers to knowing the invisible God. Our emotions need not be obstacles. Pleasure *and* pain can both be recognized as holy vessels for containing the embrace of God. Being "spiritual" doesn't require denying our sensory nature, or even our sensual nature. God made us that way.

Scripture reminds us repeatedly that God longs to draw us to his breast to comfort us, to gather us under his wings to protect us. With almost shocking passion, the Song of Songs describes the soul's love with God.

Its beginning is the most tame section:
  Let him kiss me with the kisses of his mouth—
  for your love is more delightful than wine.
  Pleasing is the fragrance of your perfumes;
  your name is like perfume poured out. . . .
  Take me away with you—let us hurry!
  Let the king bring me into his chambers.
  We rejoice and delight in you;
  we will praise your love more than wine.
  How right they are to adore you! (Song 1:2-4)

Though Solomon's Song may be descriptive of a husband and wife's love for one another, throughout history it has been also read as a description of the love affair between God and his people.

We worship and serve a God of passion. The biblical God could not be further from the Greek divine ideal, which is similar to the contemporary neopagan ideal for human life. This is summarized in the two terms *ataraxia,* which means undisturbedness or tranquillity, and *apatheia,* which is to be beyond feeling, totally at peace. In the chaos of our frenetic lives, many people hunger for ataraxia and apatheia. Books, gurus and counselors market various methods for the attainment of these elusive goals. But ataraxia and apatheia are not elusive simply because they contradict our disordered lives. They also contradict the divine order for which we are created.

We are created to be people of passion, not dispassionate, filled with feeling, not undisturbed. God himself is disturbed by the pain of his creation and rejoices over its beauty and goodness. A passionate spirituality compels those whom it has liberated to participate in the compassionate engagement of the suffering, joyful God who redemptively enters into the disorder of his broken creation, restoring it to his righteous order.

Love implies suffering. The word *compassion* literally means "to suffer with." To be able to love means to be able to embrace suffering. Thus Karl Barth writes that on the cross "God's own heart . . . suffers what the creature ought to suffer and could not suffer without being destroyed."[3] God is not apathetic, incapable of suffering, and thus dispassionate, incapable of passion. He *has suffered,* he *does suffer,* he most likely *will suffer* on our account and on our behalf.

But God is also not pathetic—feeble and helpless. God bore our suffering and took it through death into the resurrection. The cross is not the only component of the Christian response to suffering, for beyond the cross is the resurrection. There is redeemed, reconciled life in, through and after suffering.

Unless we face our feelings and there recognize and receive the touch of Christ, the spirituality of the Incarnate Lord will be walled off from us and will not fully penetrate portions of our material lives.

Seeing His Smile, Feeling His Tears

Confidence in the compassionate God frees us to know that he smiles over us in our pleasure and grieves with us in our sorrow. God weeps with those who weep and rejoices with those who rejoice. For those of us who live in a culture that is preoccupied with promoting pleasure and protecting itself from pain, this theology of passion is liberating. Pleasure can be embraced because it is good. Suffering can be embraced because it is no longer senseless. Both are sacred. In both we are given tangible ways of encountering more fully the presence of God. On the cross our suffering has been redeemed and made fruitful. In the resurrection our life has been released and made eternal.

When we suffer we need not be imprisoned in awful isolation. Paul writes, "I resolved to know nothing while I was with you except Jesus Christ and him crucified" (1 Cor 2:2). Christ is present in our pain, our fear, our weakness, bearing it with us and redeeming it.

A sense of abandonment and loneliness often amplifies the misery of those who suffer. But we do not suffer alone, for through whatever pain we encounter, we are participating in the life of our Lord at his deepest moment of agony. Further, we have the privileged role of entering into others' suffering and there finding fellowship with them and the Lord Christ.

There is only one Christian answer to the horrific problem of suffering: Christ crucified—Christ who bore, participates in and redeems our pain.

Paul's words in 1 Corinthians 2:2 indicate that his motive, goal and ambition in ministry were to know Christ crucified. His goal wasn't simply to know Christ in his resurrection glory: he also wanted to know Christ in his pain.

Paul didn't merely seek Christ in personal isolation, as the focal point of private piety. Rather, he sought Christ among the people whom he was serving. He sought to know nothing among them but Christ dying for their sins and bearing their pain and suffering. He sought Christ as the light of their darkness and the deliverer of their doubt-filled existence.

This provides a radical revision of our reason for living. Career, success, impact, significance and security all wither in comparison, revealed as triflingly tiny objectives of all our effort. We are free to find joy in all that jostles and jolts us, plagues and pains us. The gospel makes the unique claim among the world's religions that in suffering we can clearly find God.

I recently asked an elderly friend how she has been coping since the death of her husband several years earlier. She said that she still cries every day and feels a deep loneliness. But she had decided at her husband's memorial service that every day she would give him the gift of her joy.

She said, "I've discovered that sorrow and joy aren't mutually exclusive. In fact, they are my daily companions."

I asked, "What helps you choose joy each day?"

Her reply reflected the wisdom of those who have lived long. "Every day I seek to focus on one thing that's beautiful, and to do something for someone else that costs me something."

Paying the Price for Joy

It costs dearly to find true joy in our daily lives. We don't find it by insulating or isolating ourselves from the world. We also don't find it by either denying our desires or indulging them. As my elderly friend says, we find it by *focusing on what is beautiful and doing something that's costly.*

After commanding us to rejoice (Phil 4:4), Paul provides a key to joy by telling us to fix our minds on what is "true . . . noble . . . right . . . pure . . . lovely . . . admirable . . . excellent or praiseworthy" (v. 8). However, doing this requires effort. In verse 9 Paul says, "Whatever you have learned or received or heard from me, or seen in me—put it into practice."

Just as joy requires the cultivation of minds fixed on what is beautiful and praiseworthy, it also requires lives that are fixed on compassion for others. Earlier in Philippians Paul says to the believers that if there is "any tenderness and compassion, then make my joy complete" by doing "nothing out of selfish ambition or vain conceit, but in humility consider others better than yourselves. Each of you should look not only to your own interests, but also to the interests of others" (2:1-4). These verses provide us with a very workable, in fact a "hard-workable," definition of joyous compassion—looking out for the interests of others. Henri Nouwen writes,

> Let us not underestimate how hard it is to be compassionate. Compassion is hard because it requires the inner disposition to go with others to the place where they are weak, vulnerable, lonely and broken. But this is not our spontaneous response to suffering. What we desire most is to do away with suffering by fleeing from it or finding a quick cure for it.[4]

God gives us neither escape from sorrow and suffering nor a quick fix to remove them from us. Instead he gives us the gift of his presence, which frees us to grieve and celebrate simultaneously. All that touches us can be received, not as a gift from God—for much that touches us is evil— but as a gift in which we find hidden the redeeming, liberating, loving presence of God. Thus we can touch truth regardless of what touches us or how other people respond to us. Again, Henri Nouwen expresses this with simple wisdom:

> The great spiritual task facing me is to so fully trust that I belong to God that I can be free in the world—free to speak even when my words are not received; free to act even when my actions are criticized, ridiculed or considered useless; free also to receive love from people and to be grateful for all the signs of God's presence in the world. I

am convinced that I will truly be able to love the world when I fully believe that I am loved far beyond its boundaries.[5]

I'll never forget a time of prayer my wife and I had with our friend Sandy the day before she died of cancer. For years she had courageously battled the disease and its equally destructive companions, despair and doubt. I asked her, "Where does God seem to be to you right now?"

"I don't know," she replied, "but I'm in the pit."

"Do you feel God's presence there with you?" we asked.

"No," she answered quietly.

"Do you see his face peering over the edge of the pit?"

"No," she said, "but that doesn't matter. God has been so kind and faithful to me all these years that just because I'm at this life's end and I don't sense his presence, I'm not going to doubt or deny him now!"

Then we went on to pray together, and Sandy prayed for her friends and family with a passion and compassion that brought us all to tears. Sandy knew that she was loved far beyond this life's boundaries, such that the pit of cancer and even death posed no barrier to her faith.

The Delightful Spiritual Assault on Our Senses

We have seen that there is nothing too mundane to be spiritual. Everything that fills, floods or assaults our senses can be transformed by the Spirit into a sign of God's presence. God would bring to life our spiritual senses so that we can see the signs of his grace that surround us. As the light of his love shines on, in and through our lives, we perceive truth in tangible ways. "Everything exposed by the light becomes visible, for it is light that makes everything visible. This is why it is said: 'Wake up, O sleeper, rise from the dead, and Christ will shine on you' " (Eph 5:13-14).

All activity becomes a place of communion. In whatever we see, hear, smell, touch or taste we can encounter God.

As I've stressed repeatedly, everything we encounter isn't God. Rather, everything can be a place for encounter with him. Isn't this an accurate application of Paul's advice regarding food sacrificed to idols: "Whether you eat or drink or whatever you do, do it all for the glory of God" (1 Cor

10:31; also see Col 3:17, 23)? When everything becomes an occasion for communion, we approach it differently. We even act differently. There we find God's glory. Our senses and—dare we say it?—our sensuality can provide opportunities for encountering God. We can actually refer to the Christian life as the development of sensuous spirituality. Rather than a base or demeaning description, this accurately describes our unique relationship with God.

C. S. Lewis speculatively speaks of this by saying that we can know things about God and encounter God in ways that even the angels can't.

The angels have no senses; their experience is purely intellectual and spiritual. That is why we know something about God which they don't. There are particular aspects of His love and joy which can be communicated to a created being only by sensuous experience. Something of God which the Seraphim can never understand flows into us from the blue of the sky, the taste of honey, the delicious embrace of water whether cold or hot, and even from sleep itself.[6]

Such sanctified stimulation of our senses requires conscious effort on our part. It doesn't come naturally. Dietrich Bonhoeffer's instruction to his young seminarians is helpful here:

The prayer of the morning will determine the day. Wasted time, temptations which beset us, weakness and listlessness in our work, disorder and indiscipline in our thinking and our relations with other people very frequently have their cause in neglect of the morning prayer. The organization and distribution of time will be better for having been rooted in prayer. The temptations which the working day brings with it will be overcome by this break-through to God. Decisions which our work demands will be simpler and easier when they are made, not in the fear of men, but solely in the presence of God. . . . Even routine mechanical work will be performed more patiently when it is done with the knowledge of God and his command.[7]

Every mundane (earthly) moment becomes eternally significant. God is present in all we encounter. As our eyes, ears, nose, mouths and hands are opened to this truth, all we encounter is seen to be verdant and vital. We participate in God's restoration of order from chaos, his bringing the coming kingdom to bear on present brokenness.

This is precisely why we need Christian firefighters, plumbers, clerks, parents and the like. We need men and women who see their hoses, wrenches, cash registers and homes as altars: places of communion as well as self-offering. God would have us claim all territory as places for his glory, places where we and others are set free to enjoy him.

We have no better places to meet him. Life is made up of brief yet unceasing, diverse, mundane moments. Therefore we need a spirituality that equips us for short, unceasing, all-inclusive encounters with the God of Life.

We inhabit a world in which most people are overwhelmed by feelings of meaninglessness, looking for purpose and direction. Given an adequate answer to the "why" question, however, we can indeed endure any "what." Without this, the purposelessness that plagues contemporary life produces boredom with life, and even the destruction of life itself. We have the means at our disposal to overcome hunger and poverty, we may be the most thoroughly entertained people in history, but boredom is proving to be a more insidious foe than anyone imagined. Concern about the meaninglessness of life isn't the sole lament of the underemployed or the retired. In recent years many supposedly successful businesspeople have commented to me about how bored they are.

"I can't imagine simply spending the next twenty years making more money," one man lamented. "I need some new challenges."

Others have said that they see no real significance in what they do during the forty to sixty hours that they spend at work each week. In response, two friends and I have created a series of seminars entitled "In Search of Meaning at Work." The first time we offered it, we had to establish a waiting list!

I mentioned earlier my encounter with the truth of humankind's "chief end" as glorifying and enjoying God. A few years ago, while teaching in Scotland, I found that truth enfleshed in the life of the university's parking-lot attendant.

Joseph was in his mid-fifties and enrolled in a class I was teaching. During one class discussion he mentioned that before becoming a parking-lot attendant he had been vice president of a bank. Curious as to why he followed this unusual "career path," the class asked him to tell them his story.

About ten years earlier, Joseph had suffered a severe stroke. It took him two years to learn to speak and walk again. He could never return to his old job in the bank. After four years of unemployment, the only job he qualified for was in the parking lot.

He said, "It used to be that when I went to work, the door was opened for me and I was greeted with 'Good morning, sir. May I take your coat for you, sir? Would you like a cup of tea, sir?' Now no one greets me, and for several years I felt like an absolute nobody. Every day as I walked to work I felt demeaned. You professors and students would bustle around in your self-importance. I was confined to my booth in the parking lot, making sure everyone had their permits and no one parked in someone else's spot. It was utterly humiliating."

"What changed?" the class asked, nearly in unison.

"One day," he said, "as I walked to work I decided to pray. I said, 'Lord, you know how humiliated I feel by this job. My life seems so pointless and without value. I can't stand this. What am I to do?'

"Then," he continued, "I felt like I heard the Lord speak to me.

" 'Joseph,' it seemed the Lord was saying, 'I want you to be a parking-lot attendant for me. I want you to offer up that booth as an altar upon which you give your life to me as a living sacrifice.' "

"What happened?" the class asked.

"I did it," he replied. "I read in Romans 12:1, 'I appeal to you therefore, brothers and sisters, by the mercies of God, to present your bodies as a living sacrifice, holy and acceptable to God, which is your spiritual worship' [NRSV]. If that was what was acceptable and pleasing to God, then that's what I wanted. Now every day as I walk to work, I give God that parking lot and my booth as a place where I can meet God and serve him.

"And you know what?" he continued. "Work has never been the same since. I'm not alone in my booth. Christ is there with me. And that makes all the difference."

Joseph expressed a wisdom seldom found even in classrooms at the most prestigious universities. Joseph had found the presence of God in the midst of the mundane. Though diminished by the consequences of a stroke, Joseph's senses couldn't have been more alive and vital. Through his discovery that the only adequate answer to "Why?" is "Who!" and by allowing every circumstance to be an altar where he could encounter the living God, Joseph was living his "chief end." He was fully enjoying and very fruitfully glorifying God! Some of his physical senses may have been impaired by the stroke, but Joseph seemed more alive than most of us.

From the perspective we've gained through recognizing that all five of our senses have spiritual counterparts that can be vehicles for encountering God, we'll now explore the most basic way of encounter—prayer. How can a "sensory spirituality" enrich and deepen our conversation with God?

5
Talking
with the
Truth

ONE OF THE GRAVEST BARRIERS TO OUR INTIMACY WITH GOD IS THE FACT THAT we're not sure God is for us. We are afraid to draw near. We're afraid that if we pour out our hearts to him, exposing our deepest needs, he might remain silent. What horror it would be to have reaffirmed our fear that God is as impotent as we are. Or, if he speaks, we're afraid he might judge us, reject us or expose us. He might change us in ways we don't want to change. He might send us off to be missionaries someplace where we have no friends. Worse yet, he might call us to be fools for him in our own town, around people who know us.

Chester was one of my heroes in the faith. When I met him, he was in his seventies and lived with an audacious boldness. Though he was supposedly retired, he still worked part time as an attorney. His reason for practicing law, however, was a bit unusual. Chester spent his free time in a very different way from most retired people, and he worked to support these other interests. He spent several months each year in India, teamed up with Indian pastors, preaching on the streets and building orphanages, clinics and churches. I saw many photos of him stripped to his waist, shovel in hand, laying the foundation for a building.

One day I asked Chester whether he had always been so outspoken and zealous in his faith.

"No. Not at all," he replied.

"What brought on the change?" I innocently asked, not at all prepared for the reply I was about to receive.

He answered, "When I retired, I realized that never once, in all my years at work, had I spoken with someone at work about my faith in Jesus Christ. Here I was, an elder in our church, one who preached at the street mission to transients, but one who'd never spoken with his own peers. I felt bad about this and told the Lord that I was sorry.

"I felt I heard God say to me," he continued, " 'Are you willing to speak for me?' "

Chester said that he replied, "Yes."

"The reason you've never talked about me with your peers is that you're afraid of looking foolish. You don't mind sharing your faith with street people, but you don't want to do it around your fellow attorneys. Are you willing to change?" Chester felt he heard God ask.

"Yes," he said.

"Are you willing to look foolish for me?"

"Yes," was his chastened reply.

"Then this Saturday I want you to stand outside the university football stadium, by the entrance you use to go to your season-ticket seats, the entrance all your friends and colleagues use, holding a sign."

"What should the sign say?" Chester asked.

"I want you to be dressed in one of the three-piece suits you used to wear to work. I want you to look your most dignified self [and Chester could look very dignified: he was tall and dashing, with a mustache and a shock of white hair]. Your sign is to read 'Jesus loves you.' "

"But Lord," Chester said, "I would look like a fool!"

"Yes," was the reply he felt he heard.

Chester obeyed. No one came to Christ through that sign, but Chester was never the same. Boldness poured into his soul, and he blazed with a new freedom and a deep passion for Christ.

"He's Good, but He's Not Safe"

Except when we're directly confronted with evil and suffering, we want a God who's tame. We don't want him to change things too radically. Our lives might be significantly disrupted.

In the Chronicles of Narnia, C. S. Lewis provides the following pertinent dialogue. The children had just learned from Mr. and Mrs. Beaver that Aslan, the son of the "great Emperor-Beyond-the-Sea," was a lion.

"Ooh!" said Susan, "I'd thought he was a man. Is he—quite safe? I shall feel rather nervous about meeting a lion."

"That you will, dearie, and no mistake," said Mrs. Beaver. "If there's anyone who can appear before Aslan without their knees knocking, they're either braver than most or else just silly."

"Then he isn't safe?" said Lucy.

"Safe?" said Mr. Beaver. "Don't you hear what Mrs. Beaver tells you? Who said anything about safe? 'Course he isn't safe. But he's good. He's the King, I tell you."[1]

God is indeed not safe. He is not like a tame lion. But he is good. He is the God who is for us. The changes that God wills in our lives are for our wholeness, not for our harm.

When Jesus says in the Sermon on the Mount, "Be perfect, therefore, as your heavenly Father is perfect" (Mt 5:48), he is not mandating moral perfectionism as a prerequisite for being accepted by God. The word for perfect, *teleios,* conveys the notion of being complete or whole, fulfilling one's reason for living. God's will for our lives is for our wholeness and fulfillment, not for our brokenness.

God did not just say no to us, to our sin and to cosmic evil when he bore their consequences on the cross. He also said an overwhelming yes, calling people through his resurrection into new life. This passion of God, seen on the face of Christ crucified, expresses the dramatic wonder of the gospel. As Augustine says, "For there is but one Son of God by nature, who in his compassion became Son of Man for our sakes, that we, by nature sons [and daughters] of men [and women], might by grace become through him sons [and daughters] of God."[2] This occurs, as Calvin says, by Christ's giving me "as it were his own garment; he speaks for me, and it is in his name that I present myself, just as though I were he himself, since it has pleased him to be so gracious as to unite me to himself."[3]

This is the heart of the gospel's good news. As Calvin concludes, "Our whole salvation and all its parts are complete in Christ."[4] Salvation is complete in Christ! Christ is not merely the bridge over an abyss, as some popular efforts to express the gospel portray. He is not merely the means by which God and people move to communion with one another. Nor is he merely the moral example of how we are to live. He is himself the movement from God to humankind, and humankind to God. He is our life.[5]

We can dare to draw near because he has so totally drawn near to us. We are so united to him by the Spirit that, as Calvin says, he speaks for us. We're clothed in his garments, presented before the Father in his name as though we were he himself. He actually is *pleased* to unite us to himself!

It is in this context that we can best understand prayer. In the perspective offered through all the dimensions of sensory spirituality that we've explored, we can begin to approach prayer with fresh insight.

Overcoming Misconceptions About Talking with God

Even when Christians finally decide that we want to draw near to God, their prayer life is too often effectively disabled by the Adversary, who shrouds prayer with unfortunate misconceptions.

Misconception 1: Prayer as a responsibility. First among these misconceptions are perverse notions of prayer as a "duty," "obligation" and "responsibility." For many of us, prayer has become a source of guilt. Few people tell me that they "feel good" about their prayer life and that it is a source of tremendous delight and satisfaction. We need to explore why this is so.

If I spoke with my wife only because it was my duty, obligation and responsibility, we would have a very sad marriage. Actually I can't wait each day to talk with my spouse. When we are apart, I eagerly find time to call her, regardless of the long-distance charges. Sometimes it is necessary to go to great effort: finding a phone on which long-distance calls can be made, getting through to the operator, making the connection. But no effort is too great. In fact, I don't even think about the effort. I simply can't wait to talk with her. Why does prayer seem so different?

Misconception 2: Prayer as a ritual. A second perverse notion is that prayer is a religious routine in which we simply mutter memorized phrases or prepackaged statements. Again, if I spoke to my spouse each day only with the same routinely mastered sentences, we would have a miserable marriage.

I once asked a dear friend who was emerging in his faith in Christ to describe his prayer life. He indicated that basically what he did was pray something he had memorized as a child in boarding school: "Lord, I am truly sorry for my sins. Forgive me, for today I have done that which I should not, and I have failed to do that which I should. Amen."

There's something commendable about that prayer. Many of us never get around to telling God that we're sorry. However, it doesn't go far enough.

I asked him, "Have you ever heard God's reply?"

He indicated that he hadn't.

I said, "God has shouted out on the cross, 'I forgive you!' After praying your prayer, why don't you thank him for his love and forgiveness, tell him you love him and ask him for what you need today to walk with him and serve him?" Since then God has opened up a new world of intimacy to this friend.

Misconception 3: Prayer as relaxation therapy. A third disturbing perversion of prayer is to see it as merely a relaxation technique or a source of power. Of course being in God's presence will bring us peace and rest. God longs for us to encounter the rest and refreshment that are found in his presence. But again, if I came to be with someone I love only in order to relax, our relationship would be tragically limited and self-referential. God is not "tame." We dare not attempt to manipulate him to serve our needs—even if those needs are highly legitimate, such as a need for greater peace.

Surveys repeatedly indicate that the vast majority of people in our supposedly secular societies pray. When these popular prayer practices are examined, however, very often they represent efforts to find peace and power. Most contemporary Westerners tend to believe in the supernatural as an impersonal power, life as controlled by a divine fate, and the individual as being on his or her own to make the most of a fairly bad situation. Increasingly we in Western societies are being influenced by a traditional animism in which the supreme God is too remote and powerful for normal human contact. Therefore people rely on intermediaries. The current fascination with angels and "spirit guides" is but a reawakening in the West of the primordial animistic religious impulse.[6]

At the bottom of the human consciousness is the certainty, the non-empirically documentable "fact," that we are not alone. We intuitively know that we are surrounded by invisible forces, by another dimension of reality. Thus even many scientists are fascinated by ideas of extraterrestrial life (UFOs), extrasensory perception (ESP), astrological influences, invisible economic hands, forces of history and the like. In our fascination with angels, however, we betray our preference for a sweet, benign "spirit" that we can influence and encourage to come to our aid.

Fear of the dark and of passing beneath ladders is still common. So few passengers are willing to sit in row 13 that many airlines have removed this row from their planes. And did you know that in France there are more registered fortunetellers than priests?[7]

Thus when we read reports of surveys telling us that the majority of people in most Western countries would still say they believe in God, in spite of the fact that under 10 percent attend Christian churches regularly, we must exercise a degree of caution. When people say they believe in God, we must ask, "Which one?" Is it a god whom we seek to control, or the God who is trustworthy enough to command our joyful service and adoration?

Misconception 4: Prayer as possible only by the "righteous." One more perversion of prayer deserves comment. Some confine it to the purview of specialists. We've made prayer the domain of saints, "prayer warriors" and "the little old ladies of the church." "Oh pastor," some say, "will you please pray for me?" The implicit assumption behind such a request is that somehow specialists pray better, more effectively. Many pastors, needing to be needed, are all too willing to succumb. Yet surveys indicate that the average pastor in the United States has the same problems as everyone else when it comes to prayer. Busyness and lack of discipline are major obstacles in their prayer life, and half admit to praying less than once a week with their spouse![8] Of course it's right to want to pray for others, and it's right to ask others to pray for us—but not because we think our own prayers are less valuable.

I remember vividly the evening I declined the invitation to say grace at dinner while visiting at my parents' home. As the pastor in the family, I am often given this opportunity at family gatherings. Though the intent is to honor me, one time following the customary request I said, "No thank you. You are as capable of saying grace as I am." Needless to say, I created an awkward moment!

The next morning when I sat down with my parents at the breakfast table, my mom said, "Everyone close their eyes." I peeked as she pulled a beautiful, heartfelt handwritten prayer out from under her placemat. By the time she was done reading it, all three of us were in tears. A new dimension of conversation was opened up for all of us.

Being Set Free to Talk with God

What frees us to overcome our misconceptions and dare to draw near to God in prayer? I believe that one simple realization unlocks our liberation. We don't have to come before God in our own merit or virtue. We don't even have to come before him in our own name or with our own words. The wonder of the gospel is that we come before the Father *in Christ.* He is the One who prays on our behalf. Unlike human priests, whose term of service is temporary, Christ as our High Priest is a "priest forever." "Because Jesus lives forever, he has a permanent priesthood. Therefore he is able to save completely those who come to God through him, because he always lives to intercede for them" (Heb 7:24-25).

Calvin describes this with intimate clarity, saying that Jesus is the One "who should appear in our name and bear us upon his shoulders and hold us bound upon his breast so that we are heard in his person."[9] This shift of focus from ourselves as the pray-ers to Christ through the Holy Spirit as the one in whom our prayers are heard is utterly liberating. "Prayer is not essentially a work which we concoct, but the opening up of our consciousness to the work of God within us. It is the Spirit bearing witness within us."[10]

Calvin captured the essence of prayer as succinctly as anyone could: "Prayer is an intimate conversation of the pious with God."[11] Few things thrill the hearts of parents more than when one of their children, especially an adult son or daughter, says, "Mom or Dad, can we do something together today? I would just like to be with you." In many ways talking with our heavenly Father is no different. If the only time I returned to my parents' home was to ask them for a loan, to borrow some tools or to drop off my children, the quality of our relationship would be limited. We also need to get together simply to catch up and enjoy being together. So it can be with our heavenly Father.

An immediate reaction to this assertion might be "That's fine to say about human relationships, but they're visible, and people talk back. I can't see God, and prayer just seems to be a monologue. Eventually I get tired of talking with myself." I hope that all we've explored about our spiritual senses provides a ready response to this. God isn't absent, and he's not silent. Our spiritual rather than physical senses may be required if we are to "see" and "hear" him, but nonetheless we can talk together. We are surrounded by vehicles of communion—communication—awaiting only the enlivening of our spiritual senses.

At times God may seem to be "hidden" from us. But this doesn't signify a divine game of hide-and-seek. Rather, God is at work to train our senses to see, hear, taste, touch and feel him. God wants us to cultivate our capacity to taste and see that he is good.

As Calvin says, God may appear to be "hidden" so that we may grow through experience, overcome "our feebleness" and "confirm his providence, while we understand not only that he promises never to fail us, and of his own will opens the way to call upon him at the very point of necessity, but also that he ever extends his hand to help his own, not wet-nursing them with words but defending them with practical help."[12] I'm convinced that sometimes when God appears to be silent and unresponsive, he is waiting to answer our prayers so that we will learn to come to him simply because we enjoy being with him, and not simply because we want him to do something for us.

On one personal retreat I took in order to seek guidance for an important issue I was facing, I was utterly frustrated by God's silence. I walked up and down the beach, having done everything I could to "prepare" myself to hear from God. I prayed. I studied Scripture. I journaled. I was so desperate I even fasted! The time of my return to the city was rapidly approaching, and still I'd received no word from God.

I had so eagerly wanted to hear from him. I felt somewhat like a jilted lover whose beloved was on a trip. I checked the mailbox every five minutes, but it remained empty. Sadly, I packed my bag and started the silent drive home.

On the ferryboat back to town, just as I was about to dock and end my quest for God's correspondence, I finally "heard" God speaking to me. The message came through the silent embrace of two lovers on the boat's bow. Wordlessly, they enjoyed each other and the beautiful view.

Rather than merely giving guidance, God wanted to give me himself. In his embrace I could walk through the perplexing problems I faced, enjoying the view with him!

God so longs to awaken our senses and thus deepen our communion with him that "on account of these things, our most merciful Father, although he never either sleeps or idles, still very often gives the impression of one sleeping or idling in order that he may thus train us, otherwise idle and lazy, to seek, ask, and entreat him to our great good."[13]

We know that the visible, physical world is not the full extent of reality. There is a wider, deeper and more real dimension to life. In prayer we *become* more real, solid and free as we dwell through dialogue in that realm. God meets us there. As Calvin affirms, in Christ the Lord "offers all happiness in place of our misery, all wealth in place of our neediness."[14]

From this perspective, prayer is anything but an onerous responsibility. It is a passionate privilege. We don't pray simply to help God or to do our religious duty. Not to pray hurts only ourselves and others. Calvin admonishes us by saying, "Otherwise, to know God as the master and bestower of all good things, who invites us to request them of him, and still not go to him and not ask of him—this would be of as little profit as for a man to neglect a treasure, buried and hidden in the earth, after it had been pointed out to him."[15]

Prayer as Rebellion Against the Status Quo

One of the most compelling mysteries of prayer is that through our prayer the One who is Life and Truth becomes more "visible" in the lives and eyes of other people. The treasure of Christ is, in Calvin's words, "buried and hidden" from people's eyes because of their blindness. In prayer we can share in the Spirit's work of opening blind eyes.

Paul prays for the Ephesians that "the eyes of your heart may be enlightened in order that you may know the hope to which he has called you, the riches of his glorious inheritance in the saints, and his incomparably great power for us who believe" (Eph 1:18-19). Toward the end of his life, when recounting his own blinding and "eye-opening" experience on the Damascus Road, Paul says the Lord announced to him, "I have appeared to you to appoint you as a servant and as a witness of what you have seen of me and what I will show you . . . to open [the Gentiles'] eyes and turn them from darkness to light" (Acts 26:16-18).

Thus just as family conversations have many dimensions, so it is with prayer. We've noted the obvious—that it is an intimate conversation through which we speak to God and hear God speaking to us. It depends on God's opening our inner ear (or the eyes of our heart) and enlivening our other spiritual senses. But there is also a less obvious dimension of prayer that deserves comment: *prayer represents the ultimate form of rebellion.*

In prayer we confess that we're not God, and that we don't want to be.

That sounds absurdly obvious, yet tragically we live much of our lives as "pretenders to the throne." Prayer teaches us to tell the truth. Further, in prayer we confess that the world is not abandoned. It's not orphaned and left on its own. Jesus said, "I will not leave you as orphans; I will come to you. Before long, the world will not see me anymore, but you will see me. Because I live, you also will live. On that day you will realize that I am in my Father, and you are in me, and I am in you" (Jn 14:18-20).

Simultaneously, we also denounce other claimants to the divine throne. We affirm that "all authority in heaven and on earth" has been given to Christ (Mt 28:18). Paul's assertion that one of the ministries of the church is to make known "the manifold wisdom of God" to "the rulers and authorities in the heavenly realms" is striking (Eph 3:10). Few think of this cosmic dimension to our ministry.

Through prayer we engage in a rebellion against fear, greed, loneliness and chaos—and against all the powers that hold people in such bondage. We denounce all that defiles, divides and dehumanizes people and claim the reconciling, redeeming presence of Christ in their lives.

Prayer is a creative act. It is anything but passive. Real prayer is transforming, for who can be in God's presence and remain the same? It is transforming of ourselves, of others and even of situations, as we bring them through prayer into the presence of God.

By separating ourselves from the world in the solitude of prayer, we participate in the intimate, redemptive interaction God is having with his rebellious, fleeing creation. Henri Nouwen affirms that "solitude shows us the way to let our behavior be shaped not by the compulsions of the world but by our new mind, the mind of Christ. Silence prevents us from being suffocated by our wordy world and teaches us to speak the Word of God."[16]

In this light, then, we can see prayer as a battle. It isn't first and foremost our own fight. Christ has already won the victory, and through the "groans" (Rom 8:26) of the Spirit we are brought into his high-priestly intercession. Yet we do have a voice in the battle. We are to be clothed in the armor of the Spirit that we might stand, proclaim God's Word and pray (Eph 6:10-20).

Prayer is the heart and core of the witnessing, confessing Christian movement. Without it, our witness risks being superficial, inadequate and easily daunted. Prayer is indeed a subversive activity. Nouwen warns,

Our society is not a community radiant with the love of Christ, but a dangerous network of domination and manipulation in which we can easily get entangled and lose our soul. The basic question is whether we ministers of Jesus Christ have not already been so deeply molded by the seductive powers of our dark world that we have become blind to our own and other people's fatal state and have lost the power and motivation to swim for our lives.[17]

Learning to Live with Passion

We often shun prayer as being too hard. It *is* hard. It's hard work. It's anything but passive. Though it may include passivity and tranquillity, it involves our entire being: heart, soul, strength and mind; body and spirit; eyes, ears, nose, taste, touch and smell. It calls forth all that we are. Thus prayer is a passionate encounter.

Sensory spirituality restores the passion to the spiritual life. We hunger and thirst to draw nearer to God. Like athletes, we leave behind all that entangles us. We press on toward the goal. We are relentlessly curious, constantly seeking signs of God's presence, sounds of God's voice in everything that surrounds us. We are dauntlessly confident, settling for nothing less than the coming of God's kingdom and the fulfilling of God's will, here and now on earth, as it is eternally in heaven.

The capacity to pray passionately is born in solitude and nurtured in community. Solitude is the surgical operating room that is required for the deep therapy of grace. When we are alone with God, we eliminate the normal scaffolding that props up our sense of worth and well-being, or our chronic self-loathing and dismay. When busyness, possessions, friends and meetings (or the abhorred absence of these) are set aside, when books and even music are silenced and I choose to be alone with God, I expose myself as I am.

While living near Paris, I was fascinated by the French artistic passion. Even the construction scaffolding surrounding buildings under renovation was sometimes covered with tarps and then painted with artistic façades in the semblance of a finished building. We often feel uncomfortable in solitude because there the coverings are removed and our not-very-attractive, still-under-construction selves are exposed. It is precisely at this point, as Nouwen says, that "the task is to persevere in my solitude, to stay in my cell until all my seductive visitors get tired of pounding on my door and leave me alone."[18]

Undesired solitude can be debilitating, but consciously chosen exposure to it isn't. Rather, it is the key to liberating freedom. Faced with our own frightening emptiness, we are released to give ourselves more fully and freely to the grace of our Lord Jesus Christ. There we discover that we are only temporarily under construction, for through the eyes of faith we see the scaffolding surrounding our lives clothed with the life of Christ.

That image isn't fully sufficient, for not only does Christ encompass us, but Christ dwells in us and we dwell in him. In reality there is no scaffolding, there are no painted tarps. Still, exposing our brokenness is vital if wholeness is to be restored. Otherwise we may not even be aware of our need.

A friend recently broke his finger. His whole hand swelled up so much that the emergency-room doctor didn't recognize which finger was broken and put the splint on the wrong one. It was only discovered a week later that the splinted finger was fine and the broken one had been unattended. The injured finger had set itself, improperly, and thus had to be rebroken.

Proper exposure of our brokenness is a true gift. Henri Nouwen notes with profound insight that "we move through life in such a distracted way that we do not even take the time and rest to wonder if any of the things we think, say or do are *worth* thinking, saying, or doing."[19] In the gift of solitude we can be delivered from the demonic drive to define our selves by our circumstances and instead find our identity in being drawn by the hand of the Son and the hand of the Spirit into the embrace of the Father. Who are we? Not merely what is liked and appreciated or rejected and abused by others. As by the mercies of God we present ourselves before him in solitude, we are set free from being conformed to this world and are transformed so that we may prove that God's will is good, acceptable and perfect (Rom 12:1-2).

If the passion of prayer comes alive most fully in solitude, it is best nurtured in community. In Romans 12 Paul immediately goes on to stress the extent to which we are members of one another as one body in Christ (vv. 4-5). In prayer we can see beneath people's façades and view them instead as beloved sons and daughters in Christ. It is for this reason that Mother Teresa of Calcutta prays each day, "Lord Jesus, when I encounter You today in Your unattractive disguise of the Irritating, the Exacting and the Unreasonable, may I still recognize You and say, 'Sweet Jesus, what a privilege it is to serve You today!' "

We need each other to call forth from us that which is good, true and life-giving. We need each other to remind us of our true name, our true identity as beloved, adopted sons and daughters in Christ. Madeleine L'Engle portrays this with compelling urgency in her science-fiction fantasy *A Wind in the Door*. A battle for the soul of the cosmos is raging in the microscopic cells of a little boy. The forces of darkness are trying to "X" him, and all goodness, "out"—dragging them into Nothingness. The victory can be won only as his true identity is named by others and his life is filled with Being. In the story, his sister calls out, "I hold you! I love you, I name you. You are not nothing. You are. I Name you Charles. . . . I fill you with Naming. Be!"[20]

God indeed has given to us the ministry of naming. Prayer is our most potent way of naming others. Ministries of caring and affirmation are the best expressions of the fruit of this prayer.

Singing the Song of the Future in the Pains of the Present

Learning to pray at times seems as strenuous as learning a foreign language. It is a battle. However, as we base our prayer on God's promises in Scripture, we can begin to pray with greater passion and boldness. The outcome of the battle isn't uncertain. It has already been won.

Praying the solution and not merely the problem. We dare not base our prayers on ourselves, or on our own or others' needs and problems. Placing such limits on prayer is exhausting and even depressing. How often have we heard pastoral "prayers of intercession" that seem like endless litanies of disease, death, divorce and disaster. We feebly conclude such prayers by slipping into a muttered recitation of the Lord's Prayer, so depressed by the world's pain that we don't really ever expect God's kingdom to come or his will to be done. We're not even sure that God is capable of giving us our daily bread!

Prayer is fed by faith, and faith depends on the awakening of our spiritual senses. "Faith is being sure of what we hope for and certain of what we do not see" (Heb 11:1). Through this awakening we are empowered to pray the solution to the pains that surround us, rather than merely wallow in our problems as we recited them to God.

What is the solution? In prayer we proclaim God's gracious character and we sing the songs of the promised coming kingdom. As Calvin says, "Accordingly, among our prayers, meditation both on God's nature and on his Word is by no means superfluous."[21] Who God is and what his new creation will look like—not ourselves or our circumstances—should determine the shape and form of our prayer. This transforms prayer into a great adventure of naming all that is good, perfect and worthy of praise in the midst of a world dominated by evil, brokenness and shame.

I heard the songs of the kingdom sung clearly by a man I met at a dinner party. He told me that he was recently divorced, without custody of his daughter, and so distraught over the divorce that he'd also lost his job. Learning that I was a theology professor, he said that he had begun to read the New Testament, though "I'm not a churchgoer and wouldn't describe myself as a Christian."

I asked him, "What have you learned so far?"

He replied, "I've learned that my life has a lot of dead wood in it, and I'm undergoing lots of pruning. If this God of yours does exist, then I've got to be willing to trust him in all things, even if they're painful."

"That's not an easy lesson," I said. "When it hurts, it's hard to trust God."

"There's more," he said, and I felt foolish for interrupting. "I've also learned that if this God of yours exists and he's who your Bible says he is, then he's good. Therefore I need not only to trust him in all things but also to thank him in all things. I need to be thankful in the midst of the collapse of my family and my finances."

I was silenced.

"A third thing I've learned," he continued, "is that this God of yours is not only good but also forgiving. So I have to be forgiving in all things. I have to forgive my ex-wife. I have to forgive my ex-boss. I have to forgive myself. I have to forgive life itself, if that's possible, for not being what I'd hoped it would be."

In this conversation the theology professor was unquestionably the student of a "nonchurchgoer" in whom God was mightily at work. I felt like one of the crowd who had just observed Jesus' encounter with the centurion who had sent friends to ask Jesus to heal his servant. The centurion said,

"Lord, do not trouble yourself, for I do not deserve to have you come under my roof. That is why I did not even consider myself worthy to come to you. But say the word, and my servant will be healed." . . . When Jesus heard this, he was amazed at him, and turning to the crowd following him, he said, "I tell you, I have not found such great faith even in Israel." (Lk 7:6-9)

God would so fill our spiritual senses with the sounds of his goodness, trustworthiness and forgiveness that our very lives sing with unquenchable delight the songs of the future. Yet as Calvin points out, "it is strange that by promises of such sweetness we are affected either so coldly or hardly at all, so that many of us prefer to wander through mazes and, forsaking the fountain of living waters, to dig for ourselves dry cisterns (Jer 2:13) rather than to embrace God's generosity, freely given to us."[22] Prayer leads us into God's generosity.

Praying from the future and not merely for the present. It's only logical. When we intercede, we are hoping that God will so act that tomorrow will be different from today. We are praying that the promises of the future will invade the present. Thus just as our prayers need to be formed by God's character, they also need to be based on his promises. If we're not asking for something God has promised, we shouldn't demand a response. Calvin comments, "Where no certain promise shows itself, we must ask of God conditionally."[23]

In Christ the past and the future are knit together—history is wedded to eternity; humanity and divinity are united. As we've seen, he is our relationship with God. In him the dynamism of the heavenly kingdom and the drudgery of the mundane on earth interpenetrate—eternal significance is found in present time. He is our life and our future.

As our eyes are opened to behold the promises of God, in faith we become so assured of the future that we speak from the context of the future into the present. One of our problems is that we have been living time backwards—from the past to the present toward the future. Biblically, the future has already been revealed in the past. So in the light of what's been shown in the past, we actually live from the known future into the present.

This shift in perspective is transforming. We do in fact know the truth about the future. Lions and lambs *will* frolic together. Sorrows *will* cease. Injustices *will* end. God *will* dwell with his people. One day we *will* stand before God clothed in the dignity and glory of our Lord Jesus Christ. There is no uncertainty about either the world's or our own ultimate future. True, we may not know much about the next months, years or even decades. But in the light of eternity, what are a few decades of uncertainty?

With the veil removed from time, we are set free to manifest signs of the future in the midst of the present. We are enabled to live with a creative boldness. The capacity of Christians to be fully engaged in the mundane problems of this present despairing age, while living with undaunted hope, is one of the most compelling signs of the kingdom.

Hope is in scant supply, for as Walter Brueggemann says, "Clearly, the dominant values of our culture, as they are embodied in economics, military policy, and sexuality, . . . are values of hopelessness."[24] Our world is dying for genuine, realistic hope, yet few people look to the church as its source. Jürgen Moltmann's words are sadly true: "The Christian faith is losing its mobilizing power in history. Many abandon Christianity because they can find in it no power of the future."[25]

The absence of creative hope among Christians reflects a tragic spiritual blindness. As I've already asserted, the gospel does not merely speak to the world *about* the coming future: it speaks *from* the future to the present world. As our senses come alive to discern signs of God's encompassing presence, we're set free to live in tiptoed anticipation of the discovery of what God is doing. Such living precludes despair, for a faith without hope wears "the strips of heresy."[26]

The church is in its very being a sign of hope. The church proves that God has neither forsaken this present world nor abandoned the future to evil. God has moved triumphantly, redemptively, into time, establishing his reign in Jesus Christ and, through his Spirit in the church, flooding the present with the resources of the future.

Our emotional agenda need not be dictated by trauma over our guilty past or travail over our troublesome present. Future hope can break into the present, opening our eyes, refreshing our souls and restoring our song. "The power of the past, which drags everything that exists into its wasteland where things cease to exist, is broken by hope which draws the new future into the sufferings of the present."[27] Faith in Christ as the Lord of the future frees us to live with joyous hope before the lords of the present. "Without faith, hope cannot laugh, and without hope, faith cannot live and give of itself in the world."[28]

Guiding Others into the Embrace of God

How, then, do we guide others into the vibrant hope that is found in the embrace of God? Some people call this spiritual direction. Today many Christians earnestly seek a relationship with a "spiritual director." I have some reservations about this trend, and especially about programs designed to train people to be "directors." I prefer that we enter into relationships as fellow disciples of Christ, under his discipline, and as fellow pilgrims in the adventure of living more fully in the grace of God.

All of us need a fellow pilgrim, a soul friend who accompanies us in the great adventure of grace. Obviously it's helpful if this person can be a mentor, providing wisdom and insight for the journey. Though we can learn by stumbling along together, progress is more rapid if one of us already knows portions of the route. Such people can help open our eyes and ears to see and hear, can help us to observe signs of God's presence, whispers of his voice. They can help us to live life more fully. They can keep us rooted in the written Word, that our lives might be knit to the Living Word.

Clement of Alexandria described the Word of God as the "companion educator," *paidagōgos.* In Roman society this was a family servant who took charge of a child and accompanied him throughout his growing up, protecting, giving example, advising. It wasn't simply an academic role, like that of a British tutor. Nor was it a nanny role. Rather, it combined the two.[29] William Barry and William Connolly, in their work on spiritual direction, suggest that this is the role of a spiritual director.

Generally speaking, effective spiritual directors are discovered by the Christian community; they do not put themselves forward without first having others seek their help. . . . Their authority arises basically from the fact that they share in the faith-life of the Christian community as it experiences its dialogue with the Lord. This makes the director first of all a brother or a sister of the directee and provides the basic ingredient for the informal, non-hierarchic—"just two people talking"—the creative atmosphere that seems basic to helpful direction today.[30]

If that's what is meant by spiritual direction, then it seems to be very consistent with how we can best help each other. There are several key roles that we can play in guiding others on this pilgrimage.

Provoking spiritual hunger. Other than leading people into an actual encounter with Christ, the greatest gift we can give them is to provoke their spiritual hunger. I discourage people from praying for greater spiritual discipline. It's more helpful to pray for greater spiritual hunger. If you're hungry enough, you'll eat.

Our problem is that we're satiated with spiritual junk food and have spoiled our appetite. Asking the right questions, providing provocative examples and nourishing people on milk while at the same time exposing them to the solid food that is available are all appetite stimulants.

We are "just two friends talking" as we walk together the road to Emmaus. As we walk, we discover that we're not alone, for in fact we have another companion. As he talks, our appetite grows. When he feeds us, we recognize him to be the Risen Lord (Lk 24:13-35).

Clarifying the focus of our spiritual life. After provoking hunger, the next step in the pilgrimage of these "two friends talking" is to eat. We don't feast on the techniques of the experts, burdening one another with spiritual how-to manuals. Nor do we feast on imitations of one another's religious experiences. Rather, we feast on Jesus Christ—his life, his worship, his prayer, his faith on our behalf.

We indeed need help in redirecting our self-blinded gaze. We're addicted to focusing on ourselves. The word for worship used in the New Testament, *proskyneō,* literally means to prostrate oneself to kiss the feet or hem of a garment. That's an other-focused (God-focused) activity.

In worship we repeat Christ's no to all the other gods that clamor for our attention and loyalty. We repeat his no to our adoration of ourselves and our own emotional experiences. We say no to the adoration of money, happiness and security. We find his fulfillment in our life as servants, his power even in our suffering, his security in the midst of our fears.

This requires constant reminders. We so easily lose sight, hearing, taste and touch with truth. James reminds us, "Come near to God and he will come near to you" (4:8). Thus in worship it is appropriate even to talk to ourselves: "Praise the LORD, O my soul; all my inmost being, praise his holy name. Praise the LORD, O my soul, and forget not all his benefits" (Ps 103:1-2).

Expanding our carrying capacity. When my wife and I set out with a missionary doctor on a trek to a mission station in the foothills of the Himalayas, I was very embarrassed to have porters carrying our bags. I rationalized it as a good way to provide employment, a private-enterprise "public works" project. But that didn't provide much satisfaction. The porters were far smaller than I was, but their carrying capacity was extraordinary. Ten miles later, as I was panting for breath and they were moving up the steep path ahead with seemingly little effort, I stopped my self-righteous complaining about having enlisted their services.

If we are to be used by God to help others in their pilgrimage, we are going to have to allow God to expand our carrying capacity. Only one who is willing to bear others' pain can help others see Christ. Yet this requires the depth of spiritual awareness that ensures that we do not attempt to bear others' loads by ourselves. We will all too quickly feel overwhelmed, oppressed and inadequate.

God doesn't ask us to do his work in others' lives. Only he can do that. Nor does he ask us to do others' work. The porters didn't carry *me* up the mountain. God does, however, invite us into the privilege of helping others with loads that are too big for them to carry just now.

Just as the Himalayan porters had developed hearts and lungs that were adequate for carrying loads at high elevations, Henri Nouwen says we need to develop "a heart large enough to embrace the entire universe." How do we do this? "Through prayer we can carry in our heart all human pain and sorrow, all conflicts and agonies, all torture and war, all hunger, loneliness and misery, not because of some great psychological or emotional capacity, but because God's heart has become one with ours."[31]

The disciples in Emmaus ran out from their communion table with the Risen Lord. They ran as fast as they could back up the road they'd come. Instead of fleeing the dangers of Jerusalem, they returned to them as quickly as they could. Why? Their brothers and sisters were carrying loads they didn't need to carry. The two disciples couldn't wait to tell them that Christ was risen!

The vistas we saw from the mountain hospital the morning after our trek, as the sun rose over the Himalayas, were breathtaking, worth every pant I had gasped on the way up. How thankful we were for our porters. The trip was more than worth the effort. Even more valuable were the extraordinary saints we met who were serving in that mission hospital.

God would indeed open our eyes, ears, mouth, nose and feelings. There is so much more yet to come in Life than we can currently envision or imagine. In Christ our lives have already been carried to their destination. Now we have the privilege of being empowered by the Spirit to help carry others' burdens as they grow to see the view. Life is so much more full when we dare to draw near!

6
The Church:
Truth the World
Can Touch

A STUDENT KNOCKED SOMEWHAT FURTIVELY ON OUR DOOR LATE ONE EVENING.
"Come in—it's good to see you," I said. He was a foreign student at the
college where we taught in Alaska, a long way from his home, and my
wife and I were always glad to talk with him. He was from a devout
Muslim family, and his father was a senator in his West African nation.

Skipping any small talk and with a somber earnestness in his voice, he
said, "Tim, I've decided to become a follower of Jesus Christ."

Wanting to honor his dignity, and restraining my enthusiasm, I said
with equal somberness, "Have you told your father?" The social consequences of his decision were enormous.

"Yes, I wrote him."

"What was his reply?" I asked.

"Mohammed, you're an adult, and I give you permission to make your
own decisions."

I pursued this, asking, "What do you think he was really saying?"

"I guess he was thinking that I'm twelve thousand miles away and he'll have to wait to deal with me once I get back home."

"Why do you want to give your life to Jesus Christ?" I asked.

"For this past year, as you know, I've come to all your Christian gatherings. There obviously isn't a mosque in Sitka. I've observed and listened. Two things struck me. First, you Christians love Jesus in a way I've seldom seen a Muslim love Allah. All my life I've revered, respected, obeyed and worshiped Allah. But I would never dare speak of having a personal relationship with Allah like you do with Jesus. Second, I've watched how you relate to one another. I've been amazed at the ways you love one another—men and women coming from many different Native American cultures, from many different states, and even welcoming us from Africa. We speak of the Islamic brotherhood, but I've never seen my fellow Muslims love one another the way you do. I want to love God and love people in the same way as the other followers of Jesus."

God has given the church the holy privilege of being truth that the world can touch. "You will be my witnesses," Jesus says (Acts 1:8). "By this everyone will know that you are my disciples, if you have love for one another" (Jn 13:35 NRSV). He prays "that all of them may be one, Father, just as you are in me and I am in you. May they also be in us so that the world may believe that you have sent me" (Jn 17:21).

How can we so live that the world will see us and our actions and glorify God? How can we be truth that the world can touch?

Posing Questions with a Hammer

We've already seen that to be a Christian is to have taken the sacrament, to have no higher loyalty than to the divine Christ. To use the language of the early church, either one is enlisted in Christ's army through the sacrament or one is a pagan. Tragically, many of us are trying to live as Christians yet have also taken an oath of loyalty to the present age, and are thus living as pagans rather than as enlisted people.

If we are going to provide the world with truth that it can recognize and touch, then, the first call to us is to *live our baptism.* Based on his experience in Tanzania, Vincent Donovan offers an insightful comment: "A missionary facing an alien pagan culture, to be an efficient instrument of the gospel, has to have the courage to cast off the idols of the tribe, of the tribe he came from."[1] Expressing the same theme from an earlier century, Nietzsche said, "There are more idols in the world than there are realities." Our task is to "sound the idols," to "pose questions with a hammer" and see whether things taken for granted are solid or hollow.[2]

Reflecting on this task, Os Guinness proclaims, "If the church makes anything else [other than God] the decisive principle of her existence, Christians risk living unauthorized lives of faith, exercising unauthorized ministries, and proclaiming an unauthorized gospel."[3] When the world touches the church—and it can't avoid getting its hands on us—what will it touch: solid truth or hollow idols? As harsh as it sounds, the gospel of Truth does indeed "pose questions with a hammer" to see whether what we worship is solid, living and "authorized."

The "Modernization" of the Church

In our efforts to be relevant to the modern world, to "fit in," we can easily become misfits. Rather than the gospel radically redefining us, we risk being defined more by our context than by Christ. The result is hollow lives based on hollow truths that shatter under the hammer's blow.

I recently received a phone call from a man I'd never met, asking if he could take me to lunch. He had heard that I was interviewing Christians in various occupations to discern how they could be better equipped to integrate their work life into their faith. Successful in his business, well respected in the Christian community and happily married, to me he seemed an expression of our best hopes for disciples of Christ. As we talked, however, it became obvious that he perceived himself differently. He indicated that while growing up, he had observed his father and his father's friends, who were well respected professionally as well as Christians. From his perspective, however, they looked great on the outside but seemed hollow on the inside. As a teenager, he had vowed never to become a "hollow man."

"Now," he said, "in my forties, I'm successful in everyone else's eyes, but I feel like I've become that which I most feared, a hollow man." With tears in his eyes, he said, "And what's more, I don't know what to do about it."

The idol of success. Guinness notes several dominant ways in which we're prone to idolize the things of our age. First, we're tempted to make an idol of success through technique and marketing. Guinness quotes a Florida pastor who said, "I must be doing right, or things wouldn't be going so well." Would Jesus have said the same? Even more dismaying is the following statement made by a Christian advertising agent: "Back in Jerusalem where the church started, God performed a miracle there on the day of Pentecost. They didn't have the benefits of buttons and media, so God had to do a little supernatural work there. But today, with our technology, we have available to us the opportunity to create the same kind of interest in a secular society."[4]

One wonders whether Jesus might have been more "successful" if he could have benefited from our marketing assistance. Possibly he could have avoided getting himself crucified!

The idol of privacy. A second idol is privatization. We're prone to separate our religious life from our public life. I mentioned earlier my elderly friend Chester, who realized with remorse that he had consciously served Christ with his volunteer time but had never invited Christ into his work as a lawyer. We may talk and live our faith very explicitly at home and church but remain silent at work. We tend to relegate the gospel to areas of personal spirituality, private morality and corporate Christian activity, and we are hesitant about exerting its influence on public life.

When we see Christians who are outspoken about their faith in public, whether in evangelistic outreaches or in political campaigns, we often feel (possibly legitimately) uncomfortable. Is there another option?

The idol of busyness. Let's hope that other option isn't simply to add more activities and responsibilities to our lives. A third, tragically obvious idol of our age is busyness or, as Guinness says, frenzy. In the nineteenth century Henry David Thoreau remarked that he couldn't get excited about the recently invented train, for it would only make "bad men go faster." The current debates over the Internet raise the same questions regarding electronic "travel," for quite obviously alongside its positive uses it gives abundant opportunity for "bad people to communicate farther."

In the West we are indeed addicted to speed and newness. Personal computers that were unimaginably sophisticated ten years ago are now viewed as archaic and irritatingly slow. We feel so burdened by the extraordinary escalation of information to process that geneticists are working on a biocomputer chip that could be filled with information and implanted in our brains. If we wanted to access data, we would simply mentally scroll through data on the chip. Soon it will be possible to store the entire Library of Congress electronically on a few chips. Will this be heaven, or will it be hell? Guinness comments that hell will be full of newspapers with a fresh edition every thirty seconds. No one will ever feel caught up!

At this point Simone Weil needs to be heard: "To be always relevant, you have to say things which are eternal."[5] Otherwise what we say today will be out of date tomorrow.

The Paganization of the Church

The church was born in a pagan context. That is clear. Why, then, are we so astonished and threatened by the challenges that our pagan world hurls at the church today? We should be experts at dealing with paganism. But as we've seen, we are unequipped, because paganism is not only outside the church, it is also inside. This isn't a new phenomenon. Some may say that it's always been the church's first battle.

The cry against modern paganism was first uttered most clearly in the twentieth century by Emil Brunner from Nazi Germany in 1934: "The danger of paganism which menaces the Church could well be mortal. . . . The Church has welcomed into its practices and doctrines so many pagan elements which are radically irreconcilable with the Christian faith such that expressions of the true life of the Church have or almost have disappeared."[6] More recently David Bosch asserted from apartheid South Africa, "The dividing lines no longer run between 'Christianity' and 'Paganism,' between the church and the world, but through the church as well. We are all, at best, 'Christopagans.' "[7] Though I don't want to belabor the diagnosis at the expense of time spent on the remedy, it is helpful to identify some of the symptoms of our life as "christopaganisms."

The powerlessness of isolation. One of the factors that undeniably contributed to the rapid growth of the church during its early centuries was the extraordinarily distinctive quality of its life as a community, and of the lives of Christians. Though nonbelievers may not have liked Christians' theology, they could not deny that they loved one another and that they cared not only for their own poor and rejected but for those of the pagans as well.[8]

In the mid-twentieth century the Indian Parliament debated a law to render the Christian church in India illegal. Prime Minister Jawharlal Nehru issued a warning to the lawmakers, saying, in effect, "History demonstrates that if you oppose the church it will grow stronger, but if you leave it alone, it will take so much of the world into itself as to be rendered impotent."

One of the factors that render our lives impotent, powerless, is that we're left alone. Loneliness plagues the life of Christians in the West, and of Christian leaders throughout the world, as a cancer of the soul. Informal interviews I have conducted with Christian leaders have led me to the conclusion that the dominant feelings many people in the West have toward work are fear, loneliness and envy.

One might legitimately ask, is this how God created us to live? If the church lived out Dietrich Bonhoeffer's counsel, our lives would be far more healthy: "Let him who cannot be alone beware of community. . . . But the reverse is also true: let him who is not in community beware of being alone."[9]

The scandal of conformity. A second symptom of our paganization is found in the sad scandal that too few transformed lives can be found within the church. A church that preaches with great power and teaches with scrupulous correctness is praiseworthy, but if new life cannot be found within it, its preaching is without credibility. If the life of the church and those within it does not confirm its teaching, that teaching will remain sterile. Orthodox doctrine is much easier to maintain than faith that manifests itself in love.[10]

We love to speak of missions, and even occasionally of evangelistic crusades. Zealous Christians call for the evangelization of this world by the year 2000. But if evangelism is calling people to Christ and to the body of Christ, what kind of body do we have to offer people? Too often our evangelistic efforts and results are evoked simply by certain religious emotions, a sense of religious duty and of guilt about the need to support the church. Meanwhile the rest of the person—his or her body, mind, social relations, family responsibilities, and engagement in work, business and government—remains abandoned and unconverted. As a result, "in our missionary outreach, we resemble a lunatic who carries the harvest into the burning barn."[11]

The impoverishment of plenty. There is one more symptom that deserves comment. Many of us have been paralyzed by plenty. Rather than offering my own description of this malady, I will let three respected commentators provide the diagnosis. Cornelius à Lapide tells us how Thomas Aquinas once called on Pope Innocent II when the latter was counting a large sum of money.

"You see, Thomas," said the pope, "the Church can no longer say, 'Silver and gold have I none.' "

"True, holy Father," said Thomas, "and neither can she say, 'Arise and walk.' "[12]

In his provocative study *Missions and Money*, Jonathan Bonk observes that "both the institutions and the personnel of the Western Christian missionary enterprise bear powerful testimony to the absolute centrality of money. In money, they live and move and have their being."[13]

In 1934 Brunner observed, "The Church is the arms which the master of the world extends towards the world in order to attract it to himself, but his arms are paralyzed. Such is the misery of the Church that the world sees its paralyzed arms and laughs."[14] Brunner went on the say that though the world laughs at the church, at the same time it has a secret nostalgia for the church. It had hoped that the church would provide the hope and the love that the world knows very well it lacks within itself.

Renewing the Church's Missionary Worship

If paganization plagues the modern church, then it is in worship that the church most fully manifests its deliverance in Christ from that plague. The keys to delivering the church from its paralysis lie in the transformation of its identity and its expectations through worship.

A church weak in worship has little will for witness, nor does it have much to witness about. Similarly, a church with no vital community life has little witness because believers are not growing to maturity and learning to function as healthy disciples. . . . To be the community of the Spirit the church must live in the atmosphere of worship.[15]

Jesus once asked a paralyzed man, "Do you want to get well?" (Jn 5:6). The man's response implied that he thought this was a stupid question. He blamed others for his inability to get into the healing waters of Bethesda. I believe Jesus asks us the same question. Do we want to live in the hope and love of Jesus Christ? Do we want to get well?

Rather than either rationalizing our paralysis or demanding that our paralyzed churches get up walk and run into the world with missionary zeal, Jesus calls the church to look at him. It is in focusing on him, and thus it is in worship, that we are set free to rise up and walk.

Worship is the church's fundamental missionary act. The African student I mentioned earlier came to Christ by watching followers of Christ worship him. I also mentioned Henry, the scientist who was drawn to faith through a worship service. My own hunger was provoked by a mysterious secret "feast" of Welch's grape juice and cut-up French bread celebrated by high-school students. I could cite many others whom I've met who first touched Truth in the embrace of a worshiping church.

A called community. The church is the *ekklēsia*, those who are called out. The *ekklēsia* in Greek society was a community of citizens called by the town clerk to decide on the affairs of a city. The church is the *ekklēsia tou theou,* meaning that it is called by the Lord of the universe and not just the lord of a town. It is commissioned to act on the affairs of the world and not just the provincial community. Thus one could translate Ephesians 4:1 literally thus: "Walk in a manner worthy of the churching [calling] of which you have been churched [called]."

The church is radically different from all other human communities. Its calling is distinct, for it exists because of the sovereign call of God. Its very being is distinct, for it is the visible body of Christ. The regulation of its activities is distinct, for the church is fundamentally a spiritual, supernatural organism, animated by the Holy Spirit. Brunner comments that the poverty of the church is its poverty in the Holy Spirit, for its poverty in faith, in love and in hope stems from this.[16]

Nothing violates the church's being more than for it to be the domain of human manipulation as other political structures are. The church's nature is violated if it degenerates into spheres of human power, domination and dictatorial authority. The church has only one head, Jesus Christ; one will, that of the Father; and one organizing force, that of the Spirit.

The church's ability to offer the world tangible truth depends on the mobilization of its members. The entire people of God must receive and exercise the value and responsibility they have before God and one another as a kingdom of priests. If a church is a church of its pastor, it will never thrive over the long run. In fact, a church dominated by its minister is unbiblical and dangerous. Only when all Christians recognize that they are called (churched) to full-time Christian service will the church experience the joyous fruitfulness of its missionary vocation. The word from which we derive laity, *laos,* simply means "people of God." This means that even the clergy can be considered members of the people of God and thus of the laity. The full-time service of all Christians does not mean that all are to volunteer in church-related roles and ministries. The service of the people of God is far more radical and penetrating than that.

The church is the community in which all are needed, all belong, all suffer when any member suffers, all are diminished when any member is absent (Rom 12; 1 Cor 12). The church is the community where all are important and have a vital role to play in its life. This is not merely the statement of a theologian's ideal or a pastor's aspiration. Rather, it describes the actual reality of the church as the body of Christ. The call of God to the church is not "Try your hardest to conform to a high ideal." Rather, it is "Allow me to so express my life in you that you become in experience that which you really are in fact."

My wife and I once had the privilege of hosting a Japanese Buddhist priest who was studying English in our city. His temple in Tokyo had been so inundated with foreign tourists that the community had sent him to the United States to learn English so that he could eventually serve as a guide. As he described the temple complex, we could understand why there were so many visitors: it featured dozens of beautiful buildings, carefully tended gardens and ponds, and hundreds of monks.

Learning that I was a pastor, he asked, "Can I see your church?"

I was serving in a large congregation, but our building was nothing compared to his temple, with its millions of pilgrims each year. I said, "No, I'm sorry, but you can't."

"Is it because I'm a Buddhist?"

"Oh no," I assured him. "Our church welcomes everyone."

"Then why can't I see it? Is it too far away, or don't you have the key?"

"If we wanted to see our church, we would need to get in our car and drive throughout the city. We would need to visit many of the neighborhoods, schools, office buildings, hospitals and factories in the area."

"Your church is very big," he said.

"Yes," I replied. "You see, when you describe your temple, you talk about its buildings and grounds. They sound wonderful. But when we talk about our church, we talk about where the members of the church live and work."

All of us as Christians are called to a vocation. All are gifted for service. Where else in society can this sense of significance be found?

A committed community. The word used in the New Testament for "fellowship," *koinōnia,* was the ordinary Greek word for a club—sports, commercial, culinary and the like. What distinguished the early church from all other clubs was the fact that only there, as opposed to all the rest of Roman society, could you find rich and poor, slave and free, Greeks and Jews, barbarians and Scythians (which simply meant superbarbarians!), men and women—all loving one another without any, *without any,* distinction (Gal 3:28; Col 3:11). Why? Because Christ is all and in all. Why? Because they had died to themselves and put on Christ, their lives were indeed hidden in his, for he was their life (Col 3:1-4). Only in Christ can all the walls that divide us be removed (Eph 2).

Our level of communication, of vulnerability, can never safely exceed the level of shared commitment we have to one another. This kind of honesty and intimate sharing is best found in a small group fellowship. Where churches have been dynamic in ministry, where people have grown dramatically in their life in Christ, one almost always finds intimate small group fellowships. House groups were integral to the early church. We find in the book of Acts eight kinds of house meetings: prayer (12:12), fellowship (21:7), Eucharist (2:46), all-night prayer meetings and teaching sessions (20:7), evangelism (16:2), neighborhood rallies (10:22; 18:26), systematic teaching sessions (5:42) and days of discipleship (20:20; 28:17).[17]

Our worship services are usually too impersonal, formal and serious to enable or permit personal sharing. There is understandably very little opportunity for discussion, confession or manifestation of love. It is when Christians gather in their homes, intimately sharing around the Word—written and living—that they can return to the world with their lives filled with love and with a testimony of God's power and grace that is worth listening to.

To say "go to church" should mean "participate in a family reunion." When the best of human families get together for a reunion, there is laughter, games, good food and endless conversations.

The early church did not dispense with large group gatherings. I'm not suggesting that we abandon traditional church structures and rely only on house groups. Large gatherings remind us that we are participants in a mighty, victorious army. They remind us that the Christian world does not rotate around us. They can help preserve us from insularity and schism. They can guard against preoccupation with private concerns and fellowship only with like-minded people.

Martin Luther, during the early part of the Reformation, encouraged all people to participate in house groups where laypeople dispensed the sacraments. All should gather at the cathedral, he said, as an act of public testimony; but the dynamic life of the community would be found in homes.

The commitment of the community of faith provides the only antidote to the self-indulgent apathy that is destroying the soul of our culture. This committed community rekindles our sense of urgency and sets before us goals that are worthy of our humanity. Tony Campolo notes, "Apathy is the inevitable result of living in a culture that fails to provide goals that challenge to greatness." Speaking specifically of ministry with youth, Campolo proclaims,

> We in youth work have mistakenly assumed that the best way to relate to young people is to provide them with various forms of entertainment. We should instead invite our young people to accept the challenge to become heroes and change the world. . . . We must inspire young people to greatness. By helping young people see themselves as agents of God's revolution, commissioned to a vocation of ultimate importance, we can provide them with a sense of calling that generates unparalleled enthusiasm for life.[18]

A sinful community. If this third mark of the missionary church is misunderstood, it may be viewed as only a rationalization for paganism. When properly understood, however, it affirms the freedom found in the gospel. Perfection is not required for either community or commitment. Luther said it correctly when he proclaimed that the face of the church is the face of a sinner. What other preacher has ever dared to say, "Be a sinner and sin boldly"? This injunction could be misunderstood as giving permission for complete self-indulgence if it is taken out of context. But read how Luther actually framed it:

> If you are a preacher of grace, then preach a true and not a fictitious grace; if grace is true, you must bear a true and not a fictitious sin. God does not save people who are not fictitious sinners. Be a sinner and sin boldly, but believe and rejoice in Christ even more boldly, for he is victorious over sin, death and the world.[19]

We think that our sin is the barrier between us and a more dynamic church life, so we attempt to articulate more clearly the Christian moral code, hoping this will eliminate sin, purify the church and enable its missionary outreach. Wrong! We are, and will always be while on this earth, sinners. The church is a gathering of sinners, and their sins are actually a part of the life, the structures, the activities and most definitely the politics of the church. But because we don't understand this, we try to hide our sin from one another, stuffing it into our ecclesial pockets, shoving it into our bureaucratic drawers, so that we can present a clear face to one another, all the while fooling no one, for our bulging pockets, our tormented eyes and our useless bureaucracies give us away.

Somehow the miracle of the gospel—that God loves sinners, that Christ died for sinners, that our righteousness is now and only will be *in Christ*—often eludes our ecclesial grasp. We keep trying to purify ourselves rather than recognizing that our purity is found only in Christ.

Denied sin blocks our capacity to come to Christ. Confessed sin reopens our ingrown and inward-turned lives toward God so that the Spirit can adopt us into Christ and thus free us to share in his perfect humanity. Tasting the delight of life in Christ further frees us to call on the Spirit to put to death our deeds of flesh so that our lives may be more and more conformed to the image of Christ.

The recognition that we are a community of sinners keeps Christ and the grace of the triune God at the heart of our life together. It also preserves us from erecting an ideal of what the Christian community should look like and then judging and harassing our brothers and sisters into conformity to this ideal. Dietrich Bonhoeffer's words on this subject form a famous and much-needed reminder:

Innumerable times a whole Christian community has broken down because it has sprung from a wish dream. . . . Just as surely as God desires to lead us to a knowledge of genuine Christian fellowship, so surely must we be overwhelmed by a great disillusionment with others, with Christians in general, and, if we are fortunate, we ourselves. By sheer grace, God will not permit us to live, even for a brief period, in a dream world. . . . He who loves his dream of a community more than the Christian community itself becomes a destroyer of the latter, even though his personal intentions may be ever so honest and earnest and sacrificial.[20]

It is only as a community of sinners that we can live with an appropriate solidarity with the world. As Karl Barth said, the church is "the society in which it is given to men to know and practice their solidarity with the world." This means

full commitment to it, unreserved participation in its situation, in the promise given it by creation, in its responsibility for the arrogance, sloth and falsehood which reign within it, in its suffering under the resultant distress, but primarily and supremely in the free grace of God demonstrated and addressed to it in Jesus Christ, and therefore in its hope.[21]

A graced community. This leads to the final remedy for our paralyzed lives. We are not imprisoned in our badness, and to be delivered ourselves we need not attempt to separate ourselves from bad people. Often we justify denominational divisions on the pretext that we are guarding our purity. Tragically, throughout its history the church has repeatedly attempted to purify itself through separation and division—or through rejecting, condemning, excommunicating or even killing sinners. If there is no place for sinners in the church, there will no longer be a church.

Our divided churches need the liberating medicine of the truth affirmed by Bonhoeffer: "Christianity means community through and in Jesus Christ. . . . What does this mean? It means, first, that a Christian needs others because of Jesus Christ. It means, second, that a Christian comes to others only through Jesus Christ. It means, third, that in Jesus Christ we have been chosen from eternity, accepted in time, and united for eternity."[22]

The church is the one place where we can be honest, real, open and vulnerable and, miraculously, still be accepted, loved, affirmed and believed in. Grace is not mere amnesty, passive acceptance in spite of our faults. Grace is God's life, reconciling us to himself and in Christ to one another. In ourselves we are imperfect and separated. In Christ we are cleansed and united. Our privileged calling is to allow the Spirit of God to make us more and more in sight what we are in faith.

An imperfect church, made up of sinners, but where one encounters God's grace will thrive much more than one that merely proclaims a perfect idea that remains in the head of believers but is never realized in their lives. The awareness that we are a sinful church cautions us about trusting people. We know all too well how unworthy of trust we are. Yet knowing that we are a graced church frees us to love people. We know in Christ how loved we are. "Our community with one another consists solely in what Christ has done to both of us."[23] We love people not because we find them to be lovable but because they are loved by God.

The church finds its mission as the graced community. The grace of God is a seeking grace. Because we have been sought and found by the God of grace, we are compelled to participate in his seeking and finding the rest of his creation. "First and supremely it is God who exists for the world. And since the community of Jesus Christ exists first and supremely for God, it has no option but in its own manner and place to exist for the world. How else could it exist for God?"[24]

As the graced community, however, the church lives in solidarity with the world but "not . . . conformity to it."[25] The church can't say yes to the world if it can't also say no. "To be sure, the community is the people which is called out of the nations by the Word of God, which is separated from the world, which is separately constituted within it and which is thus set over against it."[26] Thus grace frees the church to live a "worldly discipleship."

> Since Jesus Christ is the Savior of the world, [the church] can exist in worldly fashion, not unwilling nor with a bad conscience, but willingly and with a good conscience. . . . Hence it does not consist in a cunning masquerade, but rather in an unmasking in which it makes itself known to others as akin to them, rejoicing with them that do rejoice and weeping with them that weep (Rom 12:15), not confirming and strengthening them in evil nor betraying and surrendering them for its own good, but confessing for its own good, and thereby contending against the evil of others, by accepting the fact that it must be honestly and unreservedly among them and with them, on the same level footing, in the same boat and within the same limits as any or all of them.[27]

This fruitfulness of graced sinners releases the church to utter continually its resounding shout of joyous triumph. We no longer have to take ourselves so seriously, for we are participants in something dramatically, fruitfully greater than our petty efforts. Can we see with Paul that the gospel is constantly bearing fruit in all the world (Col 1:6)? Mission is the church's public act of adoration of God, the King of the universe, who has established his dominion within the humanity of Christ and in which we participate through the Spirit.

Our worship and our mission are acts of proclaiming the coronation and enthronement of Christ as the Servant King of creation. This joy utterly disarms all adversaries. Fear and anger they can oppose, but joy is invincible.

Making It Safe to Be Touched

Before we conclude this exploration of sensory spirituality, it's crucial that we reflect on one final concern. What makes it safe for us to allow the world to touch us? What makes us safe to be touched? In our age, touching seems generally unsafe. Too many are touched by violence. Too many have been touched by sexual abuse, so that schoolteachers are cautioned not to hug their students or even put a hand on a child's shoulder, office workers guard their distance, and church members must be wary of giving one another "holy" kisses.

No direct contact. One fact makes it safe for us to let the world come in contact with us: it's impossible for anyone to touch us directly! What do I mean by this? It's best expressed by Bonhoeffer: "Because Christ stands between me and others, I dare not desire direct fellowship with them."[28] All our relationships are mediated by Christ. We relate to all people through Christ. We don't seek direct contact. Even our marriages are mediated. Our relationships with those who threaten us and manipulate us are mediated.

Because we have died and our lives are now hidden in Christ, who is our life, he stands between us and all other people. He is not merely the mediator between us and the Father. He mediates all relationships. Thus when people are touching us as those who are "in Christ," they are touching the body of Christ. When we touch others, it is Christ's body they are encountering.

Fully accountable contact. Christ's mediation provides both a safety and an accountability in all our relationships. First, we find safety because we cannot be ultimately harmed.

One day a Nepali woman told my wife and me about her conversion. Arrested for the "crime" of becoming a follower of Jesus, she was dragged before the police and violently interrogated.

After they had beaten her, insisting that she confess who converted her, she said, "Do you want to know who converted me? He's right here."

The police looked around anxiously, wondering which of them was the secret believer.

She reassured them, "Don't worry, it wasn't one of you. Jesus converted me, and he's here with me now. What's more, go ahead and kill me if you want. I know where I'm going when I die. Do you?"

With that the police released her, for they realized that they had no power over her.

Second, an extraordinary accountability is attached to all our encounters with others. We do not speak simply in our own name, act in our own name, fantasize or scheme in our own name. All that we do, whether we are conscious of it or not, is in Christ. More pastors would be spared affairs if they kept this truth emblazoned on their consciousness. We never speak, act or spend in our own name. "This means I must release the other person from every attempt of mine to regulate, coerce and dominate him with my love."[29] It is well for pastors also to remember that it is Christ they relate to when they are dealing with their congregation. As Bonhoeffer says, "A pastor should not complain about his congregation, certainly never to other people, but also not to God. A congregation has not been entrusted to him in order that he should become its accuser before God and men."[30]

It is not only clergy who need to learn this. I recently met the coworker of a friend of mine. I deeply respect this friend as a Christian and was curious how others perceived him at work. He has an extremely demanding job, and I asked this new acquaintance, who was not yet a Christian, his impressions of my friend. Needless to say, my spirits soared when he raved about the man's integrity, compassion and competency.

Lifting Jesus Up

Because we live in Christ, our first impulse in all relationships is to make visible the invisible presence of Christ. When my wife and I first arrived in Alaska, a Tlingit Indian woman came to welcome us with a plate of cookies and a word of advice. Since this was my first pastoral responsibility and the first advice to be given me in my new role, it has marked me for life. "Whatever else you do among us," Bertha said, "lift Jesus up. Jesus said, 'If I be lifted up, I will draw all people to myself.' "

This is the essence of Christian ministry. We seek to lead all people into the presence of Christ, so that he becomes visible to them in all their hopes and fears. In this way the Father will draw people into his embrace. Nouwen says it well:

> The discipline of leading all our people with their struggles into the gentle and humble heart of God is the discipline of prayer as well as the discipline of ministry. As long as ministry only means that we worry a lot about people and their problems, as long as it means an endless number of activities which we can hardly coordinate, we are still very much dependent on our own narrow and anxious heart. But when our worries are led to the heart of God and there become prayer, then ministry and prayer become two manifestations of the all-embracing love of God.[31]

Truth for the world to touch! That is our life and our ministry. We can never fulfill this calling simply through our own determination and diligence. It is ours as a gift of God's grace, through his adoption of us into Christ and through his enlivening of our senses so that we view all life from our position in him.

Everything we encounter becomes a place of communion. In a very real sense, everything takes on a sacramental dimension—not only as an "outward and visible sign of an inner and spiritual grace" but also a reminder of our holy vow to the Divine Christ.

Everything we see, hear, taste, touch and even smell affects us differently. We become aware that "the exclusion of the weak and insignificant, the seemingly useless people, from a Christian community may actually mean the exclusion of Christ."[32] When our spiritual senses are brought to life, nothing and no one is insignificant and useless. With our senses so enlivened, we can encounter Christ's presence in all we meet. And we can enable all we meet to encounter the presence of Christ.

David and I were driving across the Scottish countryside early one Sunday morning to lead the worship service in a rural church. David was a fine theological student with a fascinating background. He had been a shepherd for twenty years and now, in his forties, following a dramatic conversion, was preparing to become a pastor.

As we crested a hill, the sunlight broke through onto a green pasture where dozens of sheep grazed. I said to David as we passed, "That must bring back many memories."

All David said in reply was "Tim, please stop the car." I stopped, and he asked me to back up to a point opposite the field we had just passed. David quietly opened the door, walked across the road and climbed over the stone fence. As I watched, he walked to the far end of the pasture. A distressed sheep was stuck on its back, and gently he shoved it upright so that it could scramble away.

I didn't realize this until David later explained what he'd done, but unsheared sheep are so top-heavy that they can get stuck on their backs and suffocate. Unless they are set right, they will die.

David and I had seen the same field. I had admired its pastoral beauty. He had seen the one sheep out of a hundred that was in danger. He viewed the sheep with the experienced eyes of a shepherd. I viewed them with the eyes of a lifelong city-dweller. Without his sight and his touch, the sheep would have soon died.

All around us are people whose distress we may not be able to see. Often it's carefully hidden. God would give us the gift of his sight, so that we can stop, climb over the walls that divide us, gently touch others and help them to their feet.

May God set our senses free so that we can live out our privileged calling of being Truth that the world can touch.

Notes

Chapter 2: Awakening Our Spiritual Senses

[1]T. S. Eliot, "Ash Wednesday," in *Complete Poems and Plays* (New York: Harcourt Brace & World, 1962), p. 65.

[2]Augustine *De catechizandis rudibus* 26.50 (MPL 40.344).

[3]Augustine *Against Faustus* 14.16 (MPL 42.357).

[4]Emil Brunner, *The Divine Imperative*, trans. Olive Wyon (London: Lutterworth, 1937), p. 76.

[5]Edward Schillebeeckx, *Christ the Sacrament of the Encounter with God* (New York: Sheed and Ward, 1963), p. 18.

[6]Ibid., pp. 14-15.

[7]James Torrance, "The Place of Jesus Christ in Worship," in *Theological Foundations for Ministry*, ed. Ray S. Anderson (Grand Rapids, Mich.: Eerdmans, 1979), pp. 360-61.

[8]Ibid., p. 350.

[9]Ibid., p. 351.

[10]Ibid., pp. 352, 354.

[11]John Calvin *Institutes of the Christian Religion* 4.17.32; trans. Ford Lewis Battles, ed. John T. McNeill (Philadelphia: Westminster Press, 1960), p. 1403.

[12]Ibid., 4.14.6, p. 1281.

[13]Brunner, *Divine Imperative*, p. 79.

[14]Lewis Smedes, *Union with Christ: A Biblical View of New Life in Jesus Christ* (Grand Rapids, Mich.: Eerdmans, 1983), p. 59.

[15]Martin Luther, "The Holy and Blessed Sacrament of Baptism," in *Works*, trans. and ed. Jaroslav Pelikan (St. Louis: Concordia, 1955-1986), 35:34-36.

[16]Ignatius of Antioch *Epistle to Polycarp* 6.2.

[17]Cyprian *On the Unity of the Catholic Church* 5 (MPL 4.501), quoted in Calvin *Institutes* 4.2.6, p. 1047.

[18]Wolfhart Pannenberg, *Christian Spirituality and Sacramental Community* (London: Darton, Longman and Todd, 1983), p. 31.

[19]Augustine *The City of God* 10.6.

[20]*Didache* 9-10, 14, in *Early Christian Fathers*, trans. and ed. Cyril Charles Richardson

(Philadelphia: Westminster Press, 1953), pp. 285-86.

[21]Calvin *Institutes* 4.17.38, pp. 1415-16.

[22]Torrance, "Place of Jesus Christ," p. 357.

Chapter 3: Seeing God's Voice

[1]P. T. Forsyth, *Missions in State and Church* (London: Hodder & Stoughton, 1908), p. 10.

[2]Ibid., p. 17.

[3]Dallas Willard, *The Spirit of the Disciplines* (San Francisco: Harper & Row, 1988), p. 29.

[4]Ibid., p. 31.

[5]David Hume, *Enquiry into Morals*, ed. L. A. Selby-Bigge (Oxford: Oxford University Press, 1957), p. 270.

[6]Willard, *Spirit of the Disciplines*, p. 68.

[7]Oswald Chambers, *The Psychology of Redemption* (London: Simpkin Marshall, 1947), pp. 26-27; quoted in Willard, *Spirit of the Disciplines*, p. 118.

[8]M. Robert Mulholland Jr., *Shaped by the Word* (Nashville: Upper Room, 1985), p. 28.

[9]Ibid., p. 29.

[10]Søren Kierkegaard, *For Self-Examination: Recommended for the Times*, trans. Edna and Howard Hong (Minneapolis: Augsburg, 1940), pp. 76-77.

[11]William Ralph Inge, *Personal Religion and the Life of Devotion* (London: Longmans, Green, 1924), p. 18; quoted by Willard, *Spirit of the Disciplines*, p. 1.

[12]Anthony, quoted in Benedicta Ward, ed., *The Sayings of the Desert Fathers* (London: Mowbrays, 1975), p. 2.

[13]Mulholland, *Shaped by the Word*, p. 19.

[14]George MacDonald, *Life Essential* (Wheaton, Ill.: Harold Shaw, 1974), p. 49.

[15]George MacDonald, *Castle Warlock* (London: Kegan Paul, Tench, Trubner, 1894), p. 193.

[16]Lesslie Newbigin, *Mission in Christ's Way* (Geneva: World Council of Churches, 1987), p. 13.

[17]Mulholland, *Shaped by the Word*, pp. 49-50.

[18]C. S. Lewis, *Mere Christianity* (New York: Macmillan, 1952), pp. 168-69.

[19]Os Guinness, "America's Last Men and Their Magnificent Talking Cure," in *No God but God*, ed. Os Guinness and John Seel (Chicago: Moody Press, 1992), p. 112.

[20]Henri Nouwen, *Making All Things New* (San Francisco: Harper & Row, 1981), pp. 67-68.

[21]Garrison Keillor, "On the Meaning of Life," in *We Are Still Married* (New York: Viking, 1989).

Chapter 4: Smelling, Tasting & Touching Truth

[1]C. S. Lewis, *The Screwtape Letters* (1952; reprint Glasgow: Collins/Fount, 1977), p. 113.

[2]Quoted in Arthur Wallis, *God's Chosen Fast* (Ft. Washington, Penn.: Christian Literature Crusade, 1971), p. 81.

[3]Karl Barth, *Church Dogmatics* 2/1, trans. T. H. L. Parker et al., ed. Geoffrey Bromiley and Thomas F. Torrance (Edinburgh: T & T Clark, 1957), p. 446 (compare pp. 396-403).

[4]Henri Nouwen, *The Way of the Heart* (New York: Ballantine Books, 1981), p. 20.

[5]Henri Nouwen, *Beyond the Mirror* (New York: Fount Paperbacks, 1990), p. 55.

[6]C. S. Lewis, "Scraps," *St. James' Magazine*, December 1945; quoted in *A Mind Awake: An Anthology of C. S. Lewis*, ed. Clyde Kilby (New York: Harcourt Brace, 1968), p. 103.

[7]Dietrich Bonhoeffer, *Life Together* (New York: Harper & Row, 1954), p. 71.

Chapter 5: Talking with the Truth

[1]C. S. Lewis, *The Lion, the Witch and the Wardrobe* (New York: Collier, 1970), pp. 75-76.

[2]Augustine *The City of God* 21.15.

[3]John Calvin *Sermon on Galatians* 3.26-29.

[4]John Calvin *Institutes of the Christian Religion* 2.16.19; trans. Ford Lewis Battles, ed. John T. McNeill (Philadelphia: Westminster Press, 1960), p. 527.

[5]For a timeless description of God's intimacy with us, see Brother Lawrence, *The Practice of the Presence of God*, trans. E. M. Blailock (London: Hodder & Stoughton, 1971).

[6]For interesting popular studies of this, see "Angels Among Us," *Time*, December 27, 1993; "In Search of Angels," *Life*, March 1994.

[7]This has been documented in Marc Spindler, "Europe's Neo-paganism," *International Bulletin of Missionary Research* 11 (January 1987); see also W. A. Vissert'Hooft, "Evangelism Among Europe's Neo-pagans," *International Review of Mission* 66, no. 4 (1977): 349-60.

[8]See David Goetz, "How Pastors Practice the Presence," *Leadership*, Fall 1993, pp. 28-35.

[9]Calvin *Institutes* 3.20.18, p. 875.

[10]Kenneth Leech, *Praying in the Spirit: Christian Spirituality in the 1990's*, Grove Spirituality Series 35 (Nottingham, England: Grove, 1990).

[11]Calvin *Institutes* 3.20.16, p. 872.

[12]Ibid., p. 852.

[13]Ibid., p. 853.

[14]Ibid., p. 850.

[15]Ibid., p. 850.

[16]Henri Nouwen, *The Way of the Heart* (New York: Ballantine, 1981), frontispiece.

[17]Ibid., p. 9.

[18]Ibid., p. 15.

[19]Ibid., p. 10.

[20]Madeleine L'Engle, *A Wind in the Door* (New York: Dell, 1973), p. 203.

[21]Calvin *Institutes* 3.20.13, p. 867.

[22]Ibid., 3.20.14, p. 867.

[23]Ibid., 3.20.15, p. 872.

[24]Walter Brueggemann, *Hope Within History* (Atlanta: John Knox Press, 1987), p. 7.

[25]Jürgen Moltmann, *Religion, Revolution and the Future*, ed. and trans. Douglas Meeks (New York: Charles Scribner's Sons, 1969), p. 133.

[26]Ibid., p. 20.

[27]Ibid., p. 37.

[28]Ibid., p. 220.

[29]Clement of Alexandria, "Christ the Educator," ed. and trans. Simon Wood, in *The Fathers of the Church*, vol. 23 (New York: Fathers of the Church, 1954); quoted by William Barry

and William Connolly, *The Practice of Spiritual Direction* (New York: Seabury, 1982), p. 23.

[30]Barry and Connolly, *Practice of Spiritual Direction*, pp. 121-22.

[31]Nouwen, *Way of the Heart*, p. 69.

Chapter 6: The Church

[1]Vincent Donovan, *Christianity Rediscovered*, 2nd ed. (Maryknoll, N.Y.: Orbis, 1982), p. 89.

[2]Friedrich Nietzsche, *Twilight of the Idols/The Anti-Christ* (London: Penguin, 1968), p. 21; quoted in Os Guinness, *Dining with the Devil: The Megachurch Movement Flirts with Modernity* (Grand Rapids, Mich.: Eerdmans, 1993), p. 31.

[3]Guinness, *Dining with the Devil*, p. 35.

[4]Ibid., p. 38, quoting *Publishers Weekly*, February 10, 1992, p. 42.

[5]Quoted by Guinness, *Dining with the Devil*, pp. 62-63.

[6]Emil Brunner, *The Renewal of the Church*, trans. Olive Wyon (Geneva: Ed. Labor, 1934), pp. 9, 30.

[7]David Bosch, *Transforming Mission* (Maryknoll, N.Y.: Orbis, 1991), p. 370.

[8]For an excellent discussion of this, see Michael Green's work *Evangelism in the Early Church* (Grand Rapids, Mich.: Eerdmans, 1970).

[9]Dietrich Bonhoeffer, *Life Together* (New York: Harper & Row, 1954), pp. 76-77.

[10]Brunner, *Renewal of the Church*, p. 51.

[11]Bosch, *Transforming Mission*, p. 5.

[12]Quoted by F. F. Bruce, *Commentary on the Book of Acts* (Grand Rapids, Mich.: Eerdmans, 1981), p. 84.

[13]Jonathan Bonk, *Missions and Money* (Maryknoll, N.Y.: Orbis, 1991), p. 69.

[14]Brunner, *Renewal of the Church*, p. 39.

[15]Howard Snyder, *Liberating the Church* (Downers Grove, Ill.: InterVarsity Press, 1983), pp. 80, 128.

[16]Ibid., p. 40.

[17]Ten reasons for taking house group fellowships seriously: they can be (1) inclusive, (2) relational and personal, (3) encouraging, (4) welcoming, (5) lay centered, (6) application-oriented, (7) easily multipliable, (8) easily engaging the world with the gospel, (9) only minimally divisive and (10) honoring of people's individuality.

[18]Tony Campolo, *Growing Up in America* (Grand Rapids, Mich.: Zondervan, 1989), pp. 152-53.

[19]Martin Luther, *Works*, ed. Jaroslav Pelikan (St. Louis: Concordia, 1955-1986), 48:281-82.

[20]Bonhoeffer, *Life Together*, pp. 26-27.

[21]Karl Barth, *Church Dogmatics* 4/3, trans. Geoffrey Bromiley (Edinburgh: T & T Clark, 1962), p. 773.

[22]Bonhoeffer, *Life Together*, p. 21.

[23]Ibid., p. 25.

[24]Barth, *Church Dogmatics*, p. 762.

[25]Ibid., p. 773.

[26]Ibid., p. 763

[27]Ibid., p. 774.

[28]Bonhoeffer, *Life Together*, p. 35.
[29]Ibid., p. 36.
[30]Ibid., p. 29.
[31]Henri Nouwen, *The Way of the Heart* (New York: Ballantine, 1981), p. 88.
[32]Bonhoeffer, *Life Together*, p. 38.

Are you hungry
- wendys
- Happy Meal
- Bag of clothes
- DVD's
- CD's

move
head to
heart.